LUTHERAN
VOICES

On Being Lutheran
Reflections on Church, Theology, and Faith

Timothy F. Lull

Foreword by Mark S. Hanson

Augsburg Fortress
Minneapolis

ON BEING LUTHERAN
Reflections on Church, Theology, and Faith

Large-quantity purchases or custom editions of these books are available at a discount from the publisher. For more information, contact the sales department at Augsburg Fortress, Publishers, 1-800-328-4648, or write to: Sales Director, Augsburg Fortress, Publishers, P.O. Box 1209, Minneapolis, MN 55440-1209.

Scripture quotations unless otherwise noted are from the Revised Standard Version of the Bible, copyright 1946, 1952, and 1971 by the Division of Christian Education of the National Council of Churches.

The contents of this book originally appeared in articles published in *The Lutheran* magazine. They are reprinted here by permission of Mary Carlton Lull.

Reflection Questions and Afterword by Mary Carlton Lull and Patricia J. Lull

Cover Design: © Koechel Peterson and Associates, Inc., Minneapolis, MN
www.koechelpeterson.com and Diana Running.
Cover image copyright © David J. Hedlund. Used by permission.

ISBN 0-8066-8001-6

The paper used in this publication meets the minimum requirements of American National Standard for Information Sciences—Permanence of Paper for Printed Library Materials, ANSI Z329.48-1984. ♾ ™

Manufactured in the U.S.A.

11   10   09   08   07   3   4   5   6   7   8   9   10

Contents

Section Four: Our Resilient Faith

Foreword

I am delighted that Augsburg Fortress is making available this collection of writings by Dr. Timothy Lull. In many ways, the voice of Timothy Lull continues to echo throughout this church and the world. I am sure it is heard almost daily in the lives of those whom he inspired and formed as theologians through his teaching and the many lectures and presentations he gave throughout this country and the world. He has left an extraordinary living legacy in those whom he helped prepare as leaders through his teaching at the Lutheran Theological Seminary at Philadelphia and his presidency at Pacific Lutheran Theological Seminary.

Not only did Timothy Lull shape individual leaders, he was instrumental in shaping the Evangelical Lutheran Church in America's eight seminaries as one network with eight linked hubs, working together and with other partners in theological education and spiritual formation. Throughout his years of ministry, Dr. Lull was committed to and passionate about preparing leaders to serve this church in a rapidly changing, increasingly complex context.

A devoted Luther scholar and articulate teacher, Tim's conviction was that Luther could and should speak to the students and the churches of today in the same way he spoke to students and church leaders in the 1500s. Tim continually made Luther accessible to Lutherans, and Lutherans understandable to sisters and brothers throughout the body of Christ. Tim's centeredness as a grounded Lutheran theologian and historian meant that he always served as a strong advocate for and interpreter of the ecumenical agreements of the Evangelical Lutheran Church in America. My understanding of Tim's reading of the Confessions was that to be Lutheran is to be fully ecumenical and thoroughly evangelical. How fitting it is that his last call at Pacific Lutheran Theological Seminary placed him in an ecumenical setting among the schools of Graduate Theological Union.

It is difficult to describe the profound personal sense of loss I experienced with Tim's death. I deeply miss the opportunities I had to be in regular conversation with him, as well as our annual retreat with this church's seminary presidents and spouses. His presence during my conversations with Pope John Paul II and his participation in various conversations in the Vatican provided occasions for me to be immersed in the depth of his wisdom, inspired by the breadth of his vision of God's grace and mercy, and renewed by his always affirming spirit. Tim continually brought us back to Bonhoeffer's interpretation of life in Christ: being the community that bears Christ's name and also lives out its faith in lives of radical discipleship for the sake of the gospel and the life of the world.

May Tim's writings shared here be an extension of his life and ministry, even as they continue to shape our lives and ministries now and long into the future.

—Mark S. Hanson
Presiding Bishop, the Evangelical Lutheran Church in America

Section One

This Church Confesses

This series of 14 articles first appeared in The Lutheran *magazine from September 7, 1988 to May 24, 1989.*

1

Our Gift and Task

"This church confesses the Triune God, Father, Son, and Holy Spirit." (Evangelical Lutheran Church in America Confession of Faith, 2.01)

Most Lutherans sense their church is well-grounded and that it proclaims a faith deeply shaped by Martin Luther and the sixteenth century Reformation. Most also know their heritage goes back further, to the Bible, which is always the source of the church's life, and to the creeds, which Lutherans share with other Christians. The ELCA's constitution claims this faith.

In one sense, that makes the ELCA a conservative church. Being conservative means having a deep appreciation for what has been received from the past. It also means we should be slow to proclaim ourselves wiser in matters of faith than those who have gone before and reluctant to judge official teaching we have received.

If this were all being confessional means, however, Lutherans would simply repeat the same sermons and read only books from before 1546, the year Luther died.

But, in fact, the ELCA Confession of Faith uses an active, present tense verb. It does not say, "This church goes along with all that Lutherans have believed before." It says, "This church confesses."

This guards against a lazy Lutheranism, a longing for earlier centuries. Without being overly impressed with our own insight, we need to see that the Holy Spirit stirs the church in our time to make a living, personal confession of faith. We, too, must give an account of the hope that is within us.

This should not mean rushing to write new confessions for our own day. Such documents often are embarrassing within a generation because they are limited to the concerns and insights of the moment.

To be a confessor means, rather, studying the heritage—Scripture, creeds, and specifically the Lutheran confessions—to see what they teach and value highly. On the basis of that study, we must then find ways to express the faith to our time, communities, and culture.

The historic Lutheran confessions perform a good service by their limited scope. They do not equally value every ancient document, church decision, or even every word that Luther wrote. But they set priorities by pointing to what is central and enduring.

> **Testimony of the theologians**
> It is wholly erroneous to say that these confessions are not our confessions because we would not write them that way, or because we are not fully convinced of everything they say. . . . What does not speak to us or for us today may become the source of guidance and renewal for others in a future hour of the church's life." (Carl Braaten, *Principles of Lutheran Theology,* page 34)

They do not settle everything. Those who share a common faith will differ among themselves about priorities for ministry, worship styles, strategies for living in the world. But the confessions point to those things which have held the church together throughout the ages—the word of God, the Trinity, faith in Jesus Christ. Agreement on this, the heart of the faith, allows us to differ on other matters.

But does confession of the Lutheran convictions work against the ecumenical hopes of our church today? Some of what Lutherans confess sets them apart from others.

Yet, the ELCA's confession also binds us to other Christians. First, much of what is affirmed is the common Christian heritage.

Second, much of the ecumenical agreement that has been reached in recent decades has come from careful dialogue about the participating churches' historic confessions. These have provided a strong basis to discover common faith and concerns with others.

You are invited, [in this series of articles], to study the confession. You will be surprised. The history of the church is full of strange stories, human sin, and rough compromises.

But this series is written with the confidence that much of what currently worries the church is of less importance than another question: Will North American Lutherans simply tolerate their confessional heritage or rally behind it in an informed way and say, "That's what I believe too. Thanks be to God. Show me where to sign."

For reflection

1. Are there signs that the church today is caught in the laziness of longing for earlier times? How so?
2. Describe an experience in which you had to give an account of the hope that is within you?
3. To what would you sign your own name as a confessor?

2

The Strong Name

"This church confesses the Triune God, Father, Son, and Holy Spirit." (Evangelical Lutheran Church in America Confession of Faith, 2.01)

The beginning of the ELCA Confession of Faith summarizes all that will follow by stating the name in which Christians worship God—"the Triune God, Father, Son, and Holy Spirit."

This may seem a strange or difficult place to start. Despite Christians' baptism in the name of the Triune God, the doctrine of the Trinity is not well-understood or well-loved. Trinity Sunday is celebrated each year, but often only with a comment about how mysterious God is.

The ELCA confession, however, begins like the historic confessions—by boldly naming God. This is probably the only possible starting point.

Some contend, however, that the Trinity is not a scriptural doctrine. In one sense they are right. The term itself seems not to have been used before A.D. 180. But confession of the Triune God is based on scriptural revelation.

Matthew's Gospel ends with the command to baptize "in the name of the Father, the Son, and the Holy Spirit." Paul ends the second letter to Corinth with a blessing that regularly opens our worship: "The grace of the Lord Jesus Christ and the love of God and the fellowship of the Holy Spirit be with you all."

Theologians struggled to define the doctrine of the Trinity during the period of the Council of Nicaea, A.D. 325, and Constantinople, A.D. 381. Pressure to do so arose not merely from the joy of learning or from conflicts among church leaders, but from the need to understand how the church which worshiped the one God of Israel also prayed in the name of Jesus.

The heart of faith in God as triune is a conviction that God is not an impersonal first principle who cannot be known. The doctrine of the Trinity boldly claims that there is a distinction with God (three persons) and yet love and unity (one God).

This is the foundation of our claim that God is love. We know God's love is not just a passing mood because God's grace and mercy has been revealed to us in the relation between Father, Son, and Holy Spirit. The love shown us in Jesus Christ has its source in the love within God's own being.

The doctrine of the Trinity is a claim about God's inner-life. This is what makes proposals to name the Triune God as Creator, Redeemer, and Sustainer unpersuasive.

Clearly we should struggle to work past the literal understanding of masculine names for God. And "Creator, Redeemer, Sustainer" can be a refreshing change from endless repetition of "Father, Son, and Holy Spirit."

> **Voice of the theologians**
>
> "Pastors often believe that the Trinity is too complicated to explain to the laity. Nothing could be more misguided. Believers know how to pray to the Father, daring to call him 'Father' because they pray with Jesus, God's Son, and so enter into the future these two have for them, that is, praying in the Spirit. Those who know how to do this, understand the Trinity." (Robert W. Jenson, Lutheran Theological Seminary at Gettysburg, Penn., in *Christian Dogmatics, I,* page 110)

But this alternative points to God's relation to the world, not to the harmony within God's own life. If new terms are found that are in continuity with Christian tradition, they will have to be relational, not functional.

There is a further difficulty with the "Creator, Redeemer, Sustainer" proposal. The church has taught that one should not divide God up according to our experiences, so that the Father is the creator, the Son the redeemer, and the Holy Spirit the sanctifier. The whole of God participates in creation and in redemption.

You may well feel a little discouraged even after this brief examination of the Trinity. But we cannot simply throw up our hands. We must confess our faith, beginning with some decision of how to speak of God. The triune name of God is the clue to God's grace.

Our church's confession begins with a bold statement of what an ancient hymn calls "the strong name of the Trinity" (*Lutheran Book of Worship*, 188). It is the name of the God who gave us life, a name, and a reality to grow into throughout our pilgrimage of faith.

For reflection

1. The author invites us to describe the Trinity in relational rather than functional terms. What difference does it make that God loves God within the Trinity?

2. What new language would you propose to describe the relationship of God the Father, Son, and Holy Spirit?

3

Salvation in Christ

"This church confesses Jesus Christ as Lord and Savior and the Gospel as the power of God for the salvation of all who believe." (Evangelical Lutheran Church in America Confession of Faith, 2.02)

After confessing faith in the Triune God, the ELCA confession affirms Jesus Christ as Lord and Savior. It might seem like this is the first thing that should have been said, especially since the original Christian confession seems to have been "Jesus is Lord."

But by starting with the Trinity, the church makes its most comprehensive statement of faith, all that can be said of God based on what is revealed to us in Scripture. In its confession of Jesus, the confession turns to the specific way God has been shown to us.

Faith in the Trinity and faith in Jesus are not two competing centers for the faith. It was precisely reflection on who Jesus was and what he did for us that moved the church toward its Triune confession. This movement—from knowledge of Jesus to the fullness of faith in God—is one Christians still struggle to make.

Many Gospel stories can be read as accounts of a teacher, a wise and kind man, or a miracle-worker. But Jesus' death showed how much opposition his goodness stirred, and his resurrection exploded all the standard categories used to understand him.

But many, including church members, still see Jesus from a human point of view. They admire him and may even try to follow him. In some senses, he might be their Lord, but he could hardly be called their Savior.

That key word—Savior—in the confession announces that we know we need saving. Most people agree that there are many things wrong with the world. But only those who acknowledge a savior recognize that they are at the heart of the problem. Both human achievement and wickedness have been judged by the one who came in the Lord's name. All human beings are in need of reconciliation and forgiveness that can come only from God.

This is why Lutheran preachers should speak about sin a great deal. This should be done not from pessimism or just to remind everyone of all the world's troubles. But people need to know that those troubles have their root in our separation from God and from God's will.

The ELCA confession makes a powerful and surprising claim about Jesus, a claim that goes against the grain of wanting to use Jesus to make us more civilized or hard working. Jesus, as Lord and Savior, shows us both our need and how God meets that need.

Some people do not come to terms with Jesus as Savior, but others do not understand that his salvation is offered freely. As Paul wrote, Jesus is "the power of God for the salvation of all who believe." Power is the ability to accomplish something. What was accomplished in Jesus is nothing less than the reconciliation of the world to God.

Research suggests that many ELCA church members have never really heard the gospel as good news for them. They know Jesus is more than a good teacher and friend. Perhaps they even learned from Martin Luther's *Small Catechism* that Jesus is "true God, begotten of the Father from eternity, and also true man, born of the virgin Mary." But they have not been able to see the gospel as God's truth and power for their own lives. Perhaps this is

> **Voice of the theologians**
> When the word of forgiveness comes to a world bent on its own survival systems, that world is suddenly robbed of its whole reason for being. . . . We can only wait for help. We are thrown out of the stream that usually protects us. If Jesus lives, then we as old beings are through. (Gerhard Forde, *Christian Dogmatics, II*, page 96)

not surprising in a world that teaches that you can never get something for nothing.

But the gospel is not just information. It is a message so overwhelming we must hear it again and again for faith to take root in our hearts.

This is why the preaching of Christ as our Savior is the message to which the church must return again and again, Sunday after Sunday and season after season. Often just when grace is getting through to us, there is a fresh difficulty. And we may wonder, "How can I believe? How can I come to faith?" That problem is addressed in the next section of the confession.

For reflection

1. How can you express this understanding of Jesus as both Lord and Savior in conversations with your friends?

2. When have you experienced God as good news for your own life?

4

Steadfast in the Word

"a. Jesus Christ is the Word of God incarnate, through whom everything was made and through whose life, death, and resurrection God fashions a new creation.

"b. The proclamation of God's message to us as both Law and Gospel is the Word of God, revealing judgment and mercy through word and deed, beginning with the Word in creation, continuing in the history of Israel, and centering in all its fullness in the person and work of Jesus Christ.

"c. The canonical Scriptures of the Old and New Testaments are the written Word of God. Inspired by God's Spirit speaking through their authors, they record and announce God's revelation centering in Jesus Christ. Through them God's Spirit speaks to us to create and sustain Christian faith and fellowship for service in the world." (Evangelical Lutheran Church in America Confession of Faith, 2.02)

Suddenly the confession explodes into a complex explanation of the Word of God. Salvation in Jesus Christ is "of all who believe." But faith in Jesus is not something we can achieve by sincerity or struggle. Faith itself is a gift, one that comes to us through the Word of God.

Why is this section so long? Perhaps misunderstanding is likely at this point. In our society "Word of God" is likely to be heard as Bible or Holy Scripture. That is part of the meaning. But Lutherans intend something more than praising the Bible when they attribute faith to the power of the Word.

The first subsection celebrates the Word of God as the incarnate Lord Jesus Christ. It ties the power of the Word of God back to the confession of the Trinity that we found at the very beginning. The Word of God in its deepest and richest sense is our God in all majesty and power reaching out to us in love, bringing us to faith through dwelling among us, sharing our life, giving us Jesus so that we might not perish.

But the confession's second part reminds us that the Word of God also means the message about God, the gospel of salvation that is proclaimed in the church concerning Jesus Christ.

God comes to us both in law and gospel, in judgment and mercy, in cross and resurrection. We declare ourselves committed to this message in all its complexity. Only the full story can tell us the truth about God and about ourselves.

> **Voice of the theologians**
>
> Faith is a response to the God who issues the promise and who alone establishes the possibility of the act of communication. Faith is a necessary though secondary element in God's act of promise. (Ronald F. Thiemann, Harvard Divinity School, Cambridge, Mass., *Revelation and Theology*, pp. 150-51)

That truth finds us in the Word of God written in the Bible. Lutherans claim to be a biblical church in their own specific way. Lutherans turn to Scriptures for personal study or community preaching knowing already that at their heart is to be found not many things, but one thing: the saving knowledge of the Triune God revealed in Jesus' preaching.

We confess what we have learned there—that God's chief purpose has been to shower love and salvation on us, not primarily to fill us with information nor to make us moral people. These things are in the Bible too, and it is a key task of faith to see how they are related to the central message of Jesus Christ. But the confession helps teach us to see the witness in the Bible as one more form of that same word of God that existed from eternity and that has been proclaimed in the church since the day of Pentecost.

For the Bible to be the Word of God in this strong, effective sense, it cannot be a dead book—however perfect or inspired. It must be a living medium through which the Spirit moves us to believe the good news that we read there. This is why the Spirit is mentioned both as inspiring the authors and—equally important—as speaking to us "to create and sustain Christian faith."

In our celebration of the Reformation, we have been singing Martin Luther's hymn, *Lord, Keep Us Steadfast in Your Word.* Those who have pondered this part of the confession will understand that this is something more than a request for biblical preaching and study (although we probably could use renewal of those in many places today). It is a prayer to the Triune God that we might be a church strong in that word which has come to us from beyond ourselves.

We do not claim exclusive Lutheran copyright on this message. But we do insist that this word of grace is the central issue for the church's integrity—rather than church structure or moral improvement or the right Bible translation or even relevance to the needs of the day. The Word of God in all its forms—incarnate, proclaimed, and written—alone gives life to the church in any age.

For reflection

1. The author describes God's Word as incarnate, proclaimed, and written. Can you give an example of each of those in the life of your congregation?

2. Why is it important for Christians to hear God's Word as judgment and as mercy?

3. How are the moral teachings of Jesus related to the central message of the Gospel?

5

The Restless Word

"This church accepts the canonical Scriptures of the Old and New Testaments as the inspired Word of God and the authoritative source and norm of its proclamation, faith, and life." (Evangelical Lutheran Church in America Confession of Faith, 2.03)

The Bible has been central in the life of Lutheran churches. It is no surprise then that the ELCA makes clear commitments to biblical authority.

First, it accepts as "canonical" the sixty-six books of the Old and New Testaments that Lutherans and other Protestants have accepted as Scripture since the Reformation. *Canon* means rule or measurement. The ELCA affirms that these books are the inspired word of God, the measure of its life and teaching.

To many Lutherans, it is surprising that there is any question about what the Bible should include. The Bible, however, emerged slowly in the first three hundred years of the Christian church. It took some time for Christians to see how the Old Testament was the word of God for them. It took centuries before agreement developed about which early Christian writings would be of lasting authority for the church.

The church decided what the Bible would include; some books were excluded. Christians were interested in many of the excluded books. Still, the church did not find God's living word that brings people to faith in such books as Shepherd of Hermas, Barnabas, or 1 Clement. Nor did Martin Luther and later Protestants find that word in the books of the Apocrypha, written late in the Old Testament period, that still appear in the Roman Catholic Bible.

The ELCA confession next affirms both Old and New Testaments as the word of God. Some Lutherans are under the impression that the Old Testament is a secondary part of the Bible. They see it as only a law book or a history of failure and, perhaps, do not see Christ in it. This view is dangerously close to that of Marcion, a second-century church leader who rejected the Old Testament, thinking it had been replaced by the New Testament.

This was not Luther's approach. In his preface to the Old Testament of 1523 he warned: "The ground and proof of the New Testament is surely not to be despised, and therefore the Old Testament is to be highly regarded." He taught that the Old Testament was not simply law nor the New Testament simply gospel. Both contain demand and promise, judgment and grace.

But what is the ELCA's specific view of the authority of Scripture? The confession simply affirms that the Bible is "the inspired word of God."

Some Lutherans are disappointed that there is no claim that the Bible is infallible, inerrant, or non-contradictory. They believe these words emphasize the central place and power of the Bible in the church.

But it serves us well not to rush by the word "inspired" without considering its strong claim. The ELCA affirms that God has spoken and still speaks through the Bible to bring us to faith.

Adjectives are not piled up to emphasize the meaning of "inspired." Instead, the confession makes a sweeping claim about the

> **Voice of the theologians**
> "But as we ask and listen, as we attend carefully to what a given author intended to say and ponder the relevance of that message for our own times and situations, the Word of the Lord breaks into our inquiry. Through, in the midst of, or in, with, and under the rich diversity of voices in the Scripture, the living Lord speaks to us, to our times and conditions." (David L. Tiede, Luther Northwestern Seminary, St. Paul, Minn., in *Studies in Lutheran Hermeneutics*, page 292)

Bible's function. It is "the authoritative source and norm of (our) proclamation, faith, and life."

This is partly a memory of how God's word gave the church fresh insight and vision during the Reformation. But it is also a living hope that God will continue to use the Bible to shake us from complacency and call us to new life.

There is nothing automatic about this. The Bible challenges us not so much through direct instructions as through regular wrestling with its message. Our hope rests not in preserving the past but in the life-renewing encounter with the word. That is our Lutheran experience. And it is a strong confession of biblical authority.

For reflection

1. In our day, some Christians are interested in a variety of ancient texts that are not included in the Old and New Testaments. Why do Lutherans insist on focusing most attention on God's living word that leads people to faith?

2. Can you think of examples of "demand, promise, judgment, and grace" in the Old Testament? In the New Testament?

3. How do you and others in your congregation use the Bible in daily life?

6

Yardstick of the Faith

"This church accepts the Apostles', Nicene, and Athanasian Creeds as true declarations of the faith of this church." (Evangelical Lutheran Church in America Confession of Faith, 2.04)

The ELCA Confession of Faith names ten documents in which the biblical faith is clearly found. These documents were affirmed as the official teachings or confessions of the Evangelical Lutheran Church in 1580 and published in a single volume, *The Book of Concord.*

The Apostles' Creed is certainly the most familiar of the ten documents. A charming but unlikely legend says the apostles gathered after Pentecost and wrote this creed as a guide for the church, with each apostle contributing one phrase.

More likely, the creed developed in Rome, perhaps toward the end of the first century, as part of a baptismal ritual. The person being baptized was asked if she or he believed in the Father, then in the Son, and then in the Holy Spirit. Then the person was baptized in the name of the Triune God.

Over time the answers to these three questions were recited in a single creed on occasions other than baptism. The answers were expanded to include major events in Jesus' ministry to add more detail about what Christians believed. Other beliefs about the church, forgiveness, and eternal life were mentioned in connection with the Spirit.

As the creed grew in detail, its use spread beyond Rome. Eventually it was used both at baptisms and in daily worship throughout Western Europe. It has never had official status among Eastern Orthodox Christians.

> **Voice of the theologians**
>
> "The texts of the creeds themselves were far from uniform and . . . each author adapted and elaborated the texts to suit his purposes. Two elements remain constant through the citations, and one or both of them may safely be said to have formed the outline of most creeds: Father, Son, and Holy Spirit; the life, death, and resurrection of Jesus Christ." (Jaroslav Pelikan, Yale University, New Haven, Conn., *The Christian Tradition,* Vol. I, p. 1,177)

Since the Apostles' Creed was used at our baptism, each time it is used should remind us of the name and promises of the Triune God and about our identity as Christians.

The creed's current form in the *Lutheran Book of Worship,* "I believe . . ." also presses us to ask, "Is this what I personally believe?" It is healthy for us to test ourselves against this long-established community standard. At times Christians may experience real discomfort when saying these words. Some people may be puzzled or discouraged by the creed. Perhaps they do not understand the words. Perhaps they understand but are not sure that they believe. Perhaps the number of details overwhelms them.

Even at Christmas, some may experience a brief moment of concern as they approach the words, "He was conceived by the power of the Holy Spirit and born of the Virgin Mary." Questions might come to mind: "Do I believe this? Did it really happen this way? How seriously should I take my doubts about things the church has affirmed, throughout the generations?"

It is a mistake not to take such questions seriously. We each find within ourselves faith and doubt, belief and unbelief. But we can give the impression that our community has no identity and our faith has no content if we are not concerned about what we believe, or if we say only those parts of the creed about which we are personally certain.

Reciting the creed puts a helpful pressure on us to be clear about what we believe. This pressure helps us grow into the fullness of the church's faith.

So if you begin to wonder about "conceived by the power of the Holy Spirit" or "born of the Virgin Mary," consider your questions an opportunity to grow in personal certainty in the faith handed down from the apostles.

When you are troubled or discouraged by your questions, turn to the good news of Christ through which God moves us to faith.

Put yourself in the position of the shepherds, who heard the good news of Christ's birth as a great surprise. Many questions must have raced through their minds as they hurried to Bethlehem. But they rushed there because of the promise which had been spoken to them: "For to you is born this day in the city of David a Savior, who is Christ the Lord" (Luke 2:11).

For reflection

1. The Apostles' Creed is used at baptisms. How do you use this creed to strengthen your own baptismal identity?

2. What parts of the Creeds are easiest for you to say? Which aspects challenge your understanding of God?

7

Defining the Mystery

"This church accepts the Apostles', Nicene, and Athanasian Creeds as true declarations of the faith of this church." (Evangelical Lutheran Church in America Confession of Faith, 2.04)

The Apostles' and the Nicene Creeds are most commonly confessed in our worship. The major impression of the difference between the two is that the Nicene Creed is a lot longer. Therefore, it can seem like punishment when it has been selected for use.

It is worth becoming better informed. The Nicene Creed did not grow out of the baptismal liturgy. It is the product of important, formal meetings of church leaders at a time Christians were deeply divided.

This creed's basic outline was adopted in A.D. 325 at the Council of Nicaea in what is now Turkey. The Roman Emperor Constantine presided over the opening session. He had every hope that the factions of Christians who strongly disagreed about the relationship of Jesus Christ to the Father could come to some understanding.

Victory went to those who contended that Jesus Christ, the Son of God, should be distinguished from, but not subordinated to, the Father. We affirm the heart of their "high Christology" whenever we come to the words that proclaim the Son "of one being with the Father."

The creed from this ancient council is not the Nicene Creed we find in our hymnals today. It was expanded and developed over the next 125 years at the councils of Constantinople (A.D. 381) and Chalcedon (A.D. 451).

The original version ended with the simple formula: "and in the Holy Spirit." The two later assemblies developed this into the fuller statement about the person and work of the Holy Spirit that we now confess.

Our enthusiasm for the Nicene Creed should not be just a matter of respect for tradition. It instructs us about the nature of the Triune God by defining the relationships among Father, Son, and Holy Spirit.

The Nicene Creed also speaks more fully about the work of God for our salvation, reminding us of important things for which we should give thanks. The Father is maker not only of the visible world of nature, but of all of the complexity of the universe—"of all that is, seen and unseen."

> **Voice of the theologians**
>
> "The Nicene Creed in particular has acquired liturgical and expressive functions that are in some respects more important than its doctrinal use for large parts of Christendom. The act of reciting it is for millions a mighty symbol of the church's unity in space and time." (George Lindbeck, Yale Divinity School, New Haven, Conn., *The Nature of Doctrine*, page 95)

After the long and careful description of the relationship between Father and Son, the creed says, "For us and for our salvation he came down from heaven." Events in Christ's life are mentioned because of their importance for our salvation and to remind us that while the Son was "of one being with the Father," he also "was made man," fully sharing our humanity.

The section describing the work of the Holy Spirit is especially important during Epiphany when we consider Jesus' baptism, the calling of the disciples and the preaching of the kingdom of God. The Spirit is the one who spoke through the prophets, but as the book of Hebrews says, "In these last days (God) has spoken to us by a Son."

Now the Spirit calls men and women to life in the church, described more fully as "one holy catholic and apostolic Church." In that community the Spirit has led us to "one baptism for the for-giveness of sins." And in that community we wait for "the resurrec-tion of the dead and the life of the world to come."

All this is important enough to our faith to be worth the few extra moments needed to confess the Nicene Creed. The other main feature of this creed in the form we have it is the expression: "*We* believe." It is good to affirm our personal faith and also to own this public statement of our faith community.

The "we" of the Nicene Creed is the widest "we" Christians can find. For this creed has been accepted both by Eastern (Orthodox) and Western (Roman Catholic and most Protestant) Christians. We stand with many brothers and sisters who have received the gospel of the one who "by the power of the Holy Spirit . . . became incar-nate from the Virgin Mary."

For reflection

1. Look at the texts of the Nicene Creed and the Apostles' Creed (*Lutheran Book of Worship* pages 64-65). How does the picture of the Trinity in the longer creed enhance the picture given in the shorter text?

2. What are some of the "unseen things" God has made, as affirmed in the Nicene Creed?

3. The Apostles' Creed begins, "I believe," and the Nicene Creed begins, "We believe." Why is it important to be able to confess our faith personally and in community with others?

8

Judgment on Careless Belief

"This church accepts the Apostles', Nicene, and Athanasian Creeds as true declarations of the faith of this church." (Evangelical Lutheran Church in America Confession of Faith, 2.04)

Readers of this series know the Twelve Apostles probably did not write the Apostles' Creed and that the Nicene Creed was not adopted at the Council of Nicaea. So it won't be too surprising to learn that there also is a problem with the traditional name of the third creed the ELCA confesses.

Scholars no longer hold that it was written by Athanasius, Bishop of Alexandria (A.D. 296-373). He was a firm defender of many points expressed in this creed, but there was no mention of this document in Christian sources until long after his death. It is often called *Quicunque Vult,* its opening words in Latin: "Whoever wants to be saved."

Professor Jaroslav Pelikan of Yale University, New Haven, Connecticut, has suggested a better name would be the Augustinian Creed, since it defends the doctrine of the Trinity in the terms used by the great North African theologian, Bishop Augustine (A.D. 354-430). No one has solved the mystery of the author's identity, but it seems to have come from Southern France, possibly Spain, in the fifth or sixth century.

Why was a third creed necessary? A quick look at page 54 of the *Lutheran Book of Worship* reveals it is very different in format from the Apostles' and Nicene Creeds. Its basic concern is the doctrines of the Trinity and of Christ. It defines these doctrines in much more detail than the other creeds.

These details have bothered readers throughout the centuries. As it spells out the relationships of Father, Son, and Spirit and of the humanity and divinity of Christ, the Athanasian Creed seems to go beyond simple biblical faith. This creed was the product of a long struggle to speak about God and about Christ in a way that protects the gospel from all attempts to soften the wonder and the mystery of the God made flesh in Jesus of Nazareth. It can be understood not only as a learned treatise, but also as praise for the gospel.

Study reveals the creed's important role of protecting the faith we have received. But this creed contains another problem that continues to bother many who read it even after study.

The Athanasian Creed insists that one must believe just these things and in just this way. The beginning has this warning:

> "Whoever wants to be saved
> should above all cling
> to the catholic faith.
> Whoever does not guard it
> whole and inviolable
> will doubtless perish eternally."

A warning at the end is equally severe.

Why does such language bother us so? In part, it is alien to the spirit of our own age which seeks to invite people rather than to demand conformity.

Partly, this creed is a judgment of our laxity. As a church we have not always been very public about our confessional commitments. The judgment's harshness forces us to consider that we may have neglected matters that our confessions call essential for salvation.

In the New Testament, take Galatians 1:6-9 for example, Christians are encouraged to be conformed to the true gospel. This must be distinguished from all false or misleading versions.

The Athanasian Creed has been used in Lutheran worship, especially on occasions like Trinity Sunday. The danger of such occasional use is that this creed is difficult and perhaps even offensive at first glance. The effect might be to undercut respect for the confessions of the church.

> **Voice of the theologians**
>
> "Lutherans have insisted that doctrinal decisions are essentially confessional; they are the witness of the Church to the gospel in a given place and time. This means that the magisterium of the Church safeguards the eschatological nature of the infallibility of the gospel rather than the infallibility of a particular structure of the church on earth." (Eric W. Gritsch, Gettysburg Seminary, *Lutherans and Catholics in Dialogue, VI,* page 148)

So use it occasionally in worship, but only with commentary and adequate preparation. Study it in classes. But let the Athanasian Creed become better known. It binds us to millions of others who share our faith that God has been revealed in Jesus Christ.

For reflection

1. Look at the full text of the Athanasian Creed (*Lutheran Book of Worship* page 54). Many would say that the warning at the beginning is offensive to them and does not reflect a proper regard for others. What are some reasons for wrestling with an ancient creed even when its language offends modern sensibilities?

2. How might the Anthanasian Creed be introduced in your congregation so that it can be understood in a broader sense and then used in worship?

9

Claiming our Catholic Heritage

"This church accepts the Unaltered Augsburg Confession as a true witness to the Gospel, acknowledging as one with it in faith and doctrine all churches that likewise accept (its) teachings." (Evangelical Lutheran Church in America Confession of Faith, 2.05)

The Augsburg Confession summarizes in twenty-eight articles the chief teachings and reforms of the sixteenth century German Lutheran territories. These articles were presented to Emperor Charles V in Augsburg, Germany, June 25, 1530.

At that time the reformers still hoped their proposals would be accepted by the church. Martin Luther had been banished by the emperor and therefore was unable to come to Augsburg. The final drafting of the articles was done there by his colleague, Philip Melanchthon, who was noted for his precision and peaceful spirit.

Melanchthon blended two earlier sets of articles to produce a splendid confession of faith. The first part, twenty-one "articles of faith and doctrine," attempted to show that the essential Catholic faith had been maintained.

The Nicene Creed, the doctrine of the Trinity, the power of original sin, and the two natures of Christ are affirmed in the opening three articles. This leads to the central Lutheran concern-justification by faith.

Article four explains that "we receive forgiveness of sin and become righteous before God by grace, for Christ's sake, through faith." The following article affirms that the office of the ministry of word and sacrament was instituted by God to lead people to such faith.

The rest of the first part spells out key doctrines such as the church, the sacraments (with strong affirmations of baptismal grace and the real presence of Christ's body and blood in the Lord's Supper), civil government, and the right relation between faith and works.

Voice of the theologians
Protestant denominations must bring the Catholic tradition of Christianity to fuller realization and exemplify it more fully, in the same way that the Catholic side must strive to see that its own institutions are permeated by the idea of Christian freedom. (Wolfhart Pannenberg, University of Munich, *The Church*, page 98.)

The second part discusses more explosive issues—"articles about matters in dispute." Here Melanchthon tried to show that changes in church practices were made responsibly for the sake of the gospel.

Articles 22-28 discuss distributing both bread and wine at communion, the marriage of priests, the mass, confession, the distinction of foods, monastic vows, and the power of bishops.

The Augsburg Confession failed to produce reconciliation in a divided church. There was but scarce hope that the last seven articles would be approved. But even the first twenty-one, which had tried to show Lutheran agreement with Catholic teaching, were divisive. Only eight of these were accepted outright.

Lutherans rallied around the Augsburg Confession after 1530, and it became the church's chief confession as the Lutheran Reformation spread beyond Germany. It reminded Lutherans of the Catholic side of their heritage even through centuries of religious wars and bitterness. It holds a place of honor in Lutheranism equaled only by Luther's *Small Catechism.*

But the real contribution of the Augsburg Confession to Christian unity has come in our time. The Second Vatican Council, completed by Roman Catholic bishops in 1965, reformed many church practices and gave Lutherans a fresh opportunity to examine their Catholic heritage. The Augsburg Confession's claim to present true Catholic teaching has also been explored anew by Catholic theologians.

But what is meant by the statement that the ELCA affirms the *Unaltered* Augsburg Confession? There are several revised versions. In negotiations with Reformed churches in the 1540s, Melanchthon produced an amended edition that some of the Reformed were willing to accept. Some American Lutherans in the mid-nineteenth century produced an "American version," edited to make Lutheranism fit into the pattern of American Protestantism.

The ELCA, with other world Lutherans, affirms the original version presented in 1530. Its generous spirit has earned the Augsburg Confession the place of honor it holds among the Lutheran confessions.

For reflection

1. What does it mean to say that the church is catholic? What does it mean that our heritage as Lutherans is connected to the Roman Catholic Church?

2. How does the Augsburg Confession play a unifying role for Lutherans around the globe?

10

No Apology for the Faith

"This church accepts the other confessional writings in the Book of Concord, namely, the Apology of the Augsburg Confession . . . as further valid interpretations of the faith of the Church. (Evangelical Lutheran Church in America Confession of Faith, 2.06)

The Book of Concord, first assembled in 1580 in one early attempt to unite divided Lutherans, contains the three ancient creeds and seven writings from the Reformation period. If you have never seen this book, ask your pastor to see a copy.

It contains ten documents of very unequal length. The "Apology of the Augsburg Confession" is one of three longer ones. The "Apology" is a sustained commentary on the Augsburg Confession, and like that document is the work of Martin Luther's younger collaborator, Philip Melanchthon.

The Augsburg Confession's rejection by papal representatives led him to write the "Apology." Published in 1531, it is a spirited expression of what he wrote more cautiously and concisely in the Confession.

The "Apology," a strange and perhaps misleading name, suggests a backing down from one's views. But this is not at all true. The name is borrowed from some early Christian writings that vigorously defend the faith.

Melanchthon was in no mood to apologize. He wrote in the preface: "Now, I have written as moderately as I could . . . But recently, when I saw the Confutation, I realized it was written so cleverly and slanderously that in some places it could deceive even the cautious reader" (*The Book of Concord,* page 99).

The "Apology" deals with some matters briefly, but points of controversy are discussed at great length. The understanding of the church was one sharply contested point. In the "Apology," Melanchthon developed the evangelical understanding fully. While the church must have a visible structure, its unity is in the gospel, not in the uniform practice of all matters.

Melanchthon showed that the Lutherans, as they were coming to be called, valued tradition, preserved it in many places but could not ground the church's unity in it. He argued that the Roman church itself had introduced changes especially by denying the cup to people at communion. The number of sacraments may be debated. The tradition is too diverse to insist that all must agree that there are seven.

At several places where he had gone to great pains to meet the Roman objections, Melanchthon gave a detailed account of the Reformers' objections:

- Saints should be remembered, but their stories must never obscure the gospel of salvation from Christ alone.
- Bishops have a genuine calling. But the office needs reforming, as bishops are not performing their duties according to the gospel. Their true power is not in their apostolic privileges but in their service to God's word.

But the "Apology's" special glory is the long explanation of the doctrine of justification by faith alone. In the Augsburg Confession, Melanchthon carefully defined that doctrine as how we "become righteous before God by grace, for Christ's sake, through faith, when we believe that Christ suffered for us and that for his sake our sin is forgiven" (*The Book of Concord*, page 30).

Now Melanchthon spells out the doctrine's

> **Voice of the theologians**
> Justification is the act in which God accepts us in spite of our guilt, estrangement, hostility, and self-centeredness. And, in spite of our anxiety, we accept through faith that gracious acceptance of us by God. (Margaret A. Krych, Lutheran Seminary at Philadelphia, *Teaching the Gospel Today*, page 48)

biblical basis and answers objections to it. Christ is not to be under-stood as our teacher or example, one who starts us on the path to good works or to doing justice. "So it is not enough to believe that Christ was born, suffered, and was raised unless we add this article, the purpose of the history, 'the forgiveness of sins'" (*The Book of Concord*, page 114).

Then and now, people fear that such preaching leads to indif-ference to good works, and so opponents of this doctrine want it supplemented with a demand for human response.

Melanchthon stood firm against conditional justification. Such a doctrine overestimates human powers to do good works. Christian love can come only after faith in Christ. Even then the credit belongs to the Holy Spirit.

The churches that know and confess the "Apology" do not back away from justification by faith alone. It points away from our achievements to Jesus Christ. But let Melanchthon have the last word: "Therefore we conclude that we are justified before God, rec-onciled to him, and reborn by a faith that penitently grasps the promise of grace, truly enlivens the fearful mind, and is convinced that God is reconciled and propitious to us because of Christ" (*The Book of Concord*, page 166).

For reflection

1. How could you make an *apology* (a defense of the faith) to some of your friends who are curious about what it means for you to be a Lutheran Christian?

2. The place of saints in devotional life and the calling of bishops are lively topics of discussion still today. What guidance does the Apology of the Augsburg Confession give?

3. How can the concept of evangelical unity help the church deal with disagreements, factions, and divisions?

11

Things Worth Fighting For

"This church accepts the other confessional writings in the Book of Concord, namely, . . . *The Smalcald Articles* and the *Treatise*, . . . as further valid interpretations of the faith of the Church." (Evangelical Lutheran Church in America Confession of Faith, 2.06)

The Lutheran church's loyalty goes beyond the "teachings of Luther." Our confessions include the ecumenical creeds, several writings of Philip Melanchthon and the *Formula of Concord*, written by several seventeenth-century theologians.

But finally we come to a confessional writing by Martin Luther—*The Smalcald Articles.*

In the years following the attempt for agreement at Augsburg in 1530, relations between Lutherans and the Roman Catholic Church deteriorated. In 1536 Pope Paul III called for a council of the church to meet in May 1537 to settle the questions of the Reformation.

Luther was entrusted with the job of writing a list of "non-negotiables" for this council. He was well-suited for this by natural temperament and by years of writing against his opponents.

After other theologians amended them, Luther's articles were presented for the Lutherans' approval at a meeting in the town of Smalcald in February 1537. But those present were unable to support them. Luther was too sick to attend, and Melanchthon, who disagreed with the articles' harsh tone, saw that they were not adopted.

The articles became one of the Lutheran confessions only because they spoke so well for the Lutherans' deep concerns that, in the years following, they were endorsed by many Lutheran clergy. *The Smalcald Articles* capture Luther's challenge not to compromise or rest until the gospel has reformed every aspect of the church.

The first part of *The Smalcald Articles* reaffirms faith in the Trinity. The second part, which deals with Christ and redemption, states four issues on which there could be no compromise:

1. Christ and faith—"Nothing in this article can be given up or compromised, even if heaven and earth and things temporal should be destroyed."
2. The mass and invocation of saints—practices which undercut confidence in the gospel and led to merely human traditions such as purgatory, indulgences, pilgrimages, and the veneration of relics.
3. Chapters and monasteries—they must serve the needs of the church rather than claiming to be "superior to the ordinary Christian life."
4. The papacy—"the church cannot be better governed and maintained than by having all of us live under one head, Christ, and by having all the bishops equal in office."

Part III, making up the bulk of this confession, takes up fifteen issues which "we may discuss with learned and sensible men, or even among ourselves." Here Luther discusses things like sin, the law, repentance, the church, and the sacraments.

Luther's frustration with the Roman church shows through in a number of places, such as in his closing paragraph:

"Finally, there remains the pope's bag of magic tricks which contains silly and childish articles, such as the consecration of churches, the baptism of bells, the baptism of altar stones. . . . Such frauds, which are without number, we commend for adoration to their god and to themselves until they tire of them. We do not wish to have anything to do with them."

At other moments, Luther's language powerfully captures the heart of the Reformation. He wrote, for example, that the gospel

> **Voice of the theologians**
> "Since, according to Luther, the Christians constitute only a small minority among the nations of the world, practical norms for society cannot be norms that are meaningful to Christians alone. For this reason, God deals with the Christians through His means of grace, the Word, and the Sacraments, but He deals with men in general through the natural orders as they shape nature and history." (George W. Forell, University of Iowa, Iowa City, *Faith Active in Love*, page 145.)

comes to us in many ways—the spoken word, baptism, the sacrament of the altar, the power of the keys, and the mutual conversation and consolation of Christians.

The ELCA confession also affirms the *Treatise*, more commonly known as the *Treatise on the Power and Primacy of the Pope*. Melanchthon wrote the *Treatise* at the Smalcald meeting to summarize Lutheran objections to the papacy. It is sharply critical, equating the papacy with the Antichrist. Sadly, some Lutherans still hold to this identification, even after many reforms within the Roman Catholic Church.

The Smalcald Articles and the *Treatise* vigorously express what the divisions between Lutherans and the Roman church were really about. Until the task of reforming the church by the gospel is fully achieved, they will call us to those parts of our evangelical heritage that are worth a fight.

For reflection

1. What do you consider so significant that it must be reformed in order for the gospel to shine forth in our day?

2. Are these criticisms of the Roman Catholic Church still applicable today? Do they fit with your own experiences with Roman Catholic neighbors and family members?

12

Small in Name Only

"This church accepts the other confessional writings in the *Book of Concord*, namely, . . . the *Small Catechism*, the *Large Catechism*, . . . as further valid interpretations of the faith of the Church." (Evangelical Lutheran Church in America Confession of Faith, 2.06)

Some people believe that all was well with the sixteenth century church except for corruption at the official level. But when Martin Luther visited rural parishes in Saxony in 1528, he was shocked by what he found. One can still hear his disappointment:

> Good God, what wretchedness I beheld! The common people, especially those who live in the country, have no knowledge whatever of Christian teaching, and unfortunately many pastors are quite incompetent and unfitted for teaching. Although the people are supposed to be Christian, are baptized, and receive the holy sacrament, they do not know the Lord's Prayer, the Creed, or the Ten Commandments, they live as if they were pigs and irrational beasts, and now that the Gospel has been restored they have mastered the fine art of abusing liberty (*Book of Concord*, page 338).

Luther's shock set him to work in a wonderfully creative way. He wrote two catechisms: a small one for instruction of the people and a large catechism—five times as long—with more detailed information for pastors and teachers. Both were published in 1529.

Although Luther is often remembered for his controversial writings, he had a great gift for simple preaching and teaching. In the catechisms, he uses traditional materials—Ten Commandments, the Apostles' Creed, Lord's Prayer, and sacraments. But he renews our understanding of these familiar things with grace-centered theology and a fresh way of speaking.

The catechisms deserve a series of articles themselves, but it is possible to mention a few highlights. Luther begins his discussion of the first commandment in the *Large Catechism* by arguing that the real question is not whether God exists but which god we are backing. "That to which your heart clings and entrusts itself is, I say, really your God," he wrote.

The Ten Commandments speak of our relationship to the God of the Bible. Each one shows both the negative and positive meanings of fearing, loving, and trusting God above all things. Although the commandments remind us of our Creator's goodness, they also set our sin before us in a way that drives us to Christ.

Even in the shorter catechism there are many important affirmations:

Jesus, described in such careful theological terms in the creeds, is confessed more personally as "my Lord, who has redeemed me a lost and condemned creature, delivered me and freed me from all sins, from death, and from the power of the devil."

We are connected to Christ in our baptism, which is not simply water, but water connected with the promise of God's word. In the Lord's Supper, we receive "the true body and blood of our Lord Jesus Christ, under the bread and wine."

Our salvation rests in God's promise and gift. We cannot even achieve our own faith. In one of the most powerful statements of justification by faith, Luther taught: "I believe that by my own reason or strength I

> **Voice of the theologians**
> "In recent years there has been a tendency to discard the familiar catechisms of the Reformation period. That these products of sixteenth century . . . peasant life need rephrasing and re-emphasis is obvious. But casual dismissal of them by the church . . . has been detrimental to the life of the church." (Martin E. Marty, University of Chicago, *The Hidden Discipline*, page xv)

cannot believe in Jesus Christ, my Lord, or come to him. But the Holy Spirit has called me through the Gospel." God's Spirit continues to gather the church and is the powerful secret of its life.

It is hard to overstate the influence of Luther's catechisms on the church. Other documents have risen and fallen in popularity, but the catechisms have always been a central clue to what Lutherans confess.

The *Large Catechism* takes up theological controversies, but in the *Small Catechism* Luther so clearly articulated the common Christian faith that this catechism has had influence beyond Lutheranism.

It therefore seems sad that the ELCA confession did not give the *Small Catechism* a place of prominence, a separate section, like it gives the Augsburg Confession. Perhaps this is a sign of that confession's current ecumenical importance. But the *Small Catechism* complements the Augsburg Confession as Luther complements Philip Melanchthon and as parish teaching completes formal theology.

We need to remember how much we owe the *Small Catechism* and affirm it in a stronger way than just as a "further valid interpretation" of the church's faith.

For reflection

1. How are the *Small Catechism* and the *Large Catechism* used in your congregation?

2. How did you learn the basic teachings of the Christian faith?

3. To what does your own heart cling?

13

Formula for Unity

"This church accepts the other confessional writings in *The Book of Concord*, namely, . . . *The Formula of Concord*, as further valid interpretations of the faith of the Church." (Evangelical Lutheran Church in America Confession of Faith, 2.06)

Things did not go well for the Lutherans after Martin Luther's death in 1546. There were great political and theological pressures to compromise. Roman Catholics developed new unity and countered the Reformation at the Council of Trent (1545-1563). The influence of Reformed theology continued to grow, powered by the brilliant writing of John Calvin of Geneva.

Philip Melanchthon explored reconciliation with both the Reformed and Catholic churches at endless meetings, while "hardline" followers of Luther opposed these initiatives and developed his views in extreme directions. The situation further deteriorated after Melanchthon's death in 1560. Lutherans did greater damage to themselves through internal quarrels than their opponents inflicted from the outside.

The final document of the ELCA's confession, the Formula of Concord, is the result of long struggles for unity during this period. *The Formula* was drawn up in March 1577 under the leadership of a new generation of theologians, especially Jacob Andreae and Martin Chemnitz.

This confession is a long document which takes up under twelve headings the issues that Lutherans had heatedly debated. These include many topics that have continued to stir up controversy among Lutherans—original sin, free will, good works, law and gospel, and the third function or use of the law (to spur Christians to good works).

The Formula tends not to settle such matters but sets boundaries for debate. For example, the authors insist, with the Augsburg Confession, that original sin is "not a slight corruption of human nature." But against extremists who taught that humanity's fall into sin canceled the goodness of creation, it warns, "Even after the fall our nature is and remains a creature of God."

This confession also takes up controversies which developed with the Reformed churches through the fifty years since Luther's debate with theologian Ulrich Zwingli. Sections 7, 8, and 11 discuss the "Holy Supper of Christ," the "Person of Christ," and "God's Eternal Foreknowledge and Election."

Other sections deal with optional church practices and condemnations of the teachings of groups like the Anabaptists and Anti-Trinitarians.

In general, *The Formula* tries to protect the mystery of God by rightly confessing each doctrine without reducing it too neatly to a definition. Thus, the section on the Lord's Supper ends with a frequent refrain in *The Book of Concord:* "Here we take our intellect captive in obedience to Christ, as we do in other articles also, and accept this mystery in no other way than by faith and as it is revealed in the Word" (page 486).

The Formula produced its desired result in Germany—Lutherans rallied around it and reunited. It was eventually accepted by popular acclaim in Sweden and Finland. But royal opposition in Norway and Denmark led to its rejection.

Still, *The Formula's* publication spurred the collection of all Lutheran confessional writings into what we now know as *The Book of Concord.* The ten confessions, which we have been exploring, were first published under one cover on June 25, 1580, the fiftieth anniversary of the presentation of the Augsburg Confession.

The Formula's strength is that it showed the Lutherans' capacity for new theological work after the death of their first leaders. It has many quotations from Luther and the earlier confessional writings, but it has its own approach, themes and contribution. Although it has been in some ways the least known Lutheran confessional writing, it has received fresh attention in this century as Lutherans seek a fresh understanding of their identity between Roman Catholics and Calvinists.

This confession represents the first of many times Lutherans have struggled to find unity after a split. *The Formula* is a rather grim prophecy of what became a very unhappy side of later Lutheran history—a growing list of theological problems with no structural way to resolve them except to form separate churches.

For reflection

1. What do you propose as the "boundaries for debate" in the church today?

2. Published thirty-four years after Martin Luther's death, *The Formula of Concord* illustrates the Lutheran Church's capacity for new theological work. What fresh theological questions would you put before the church today?

14

Power for Mission

"This church confesses the Gospel, recorded in the Holy
Scriptures and confesses in the ecumenical creeds and Lutheran
confessional writings, as the power of God to create and sustain
the church for God's mission in the world. (Evangelical Lutheran
Church in America Confession of Faith, 2.07)

The end of the ELCA's list of confessional doctrines and documents
contains a surprise. It claims that the shape of our faith is the key to
mission. The gospel proclaimed in the Scriptures, confessed in the
creeds, and sharply defined in the confessions is the power for inclusive mission, social justice, and Christian unity.

Some doubt this today. To many, the vision of faith celebrated
in the confession seems dated, trapped in ancient philosophical concepts and sixteenth-century language. To others the notion that the
church needs a particular theology is a problem. They advocate a
practical, service-oriented Christianity.

How can the Lutheran witness to the common Christian faith
be "the power of the God to create and sustain the Church for mission in the world"?

Part of the answer is found when one understands justification
by faith, the central Lutheran way of stating the radical "gift-char-
acter" of God's love. First and foremost this redefines our relationship with God. It tells us that we cannot find our way to God by
human effort. In Christ, God has found us.

This changes our relationship to others. Those who have been
grafted into God's community by divine mercy learn that every
other human being has just as strong a claim to be God's child.
Those who understand what has happened to and for them in Jesus

Christ are purged of the pride that keeps others at a distance. They hope for a community that breaks down the walls that separate people from each other.

The same dynamic is found in baptism, Scripture, creeds, and the confessions. From an individual focus, one might be tempted to see baptism as a cosmic insurance policy. This is partly right. Those who have died and risen to new life in baptism know that nothing can separate them from God's love.

But this understanding is incomplete. Martin Luther's catechisms teach that, although our life in the world is demanding and although we fail again and again, our baptism allows us to rise each day to new life with fresh praise of God on our lips and renewed opportunities for service.

When baptism is understood this way, the church is not seen as a consumer club where people go to get salvation. The church becomes "a chosen race, a royal priesthood, a holy nation, God's own people" (1 Peter 2:9). Each Christian is challenged to be an active part of the mission of God's people.

So our doctrines are rightly proclaimed not just as personal good news but also as the key to mission and service. In such faith one discovers a power to sustain a commitment that greatly exceeds our own capacity to care.

Part of the difficulty of mission today is that we are facing deep problems that involve long years of struggle. How can a person have the compassion or commitment for mission when results are slow and needs overwhelming? Neither social justice, racial harmony, Christian unity, or world peace are likely to be achieved in one generation by a single burst of mission energy.

> **Voice of the theologians**
>
> "It is in the church that we receive the clearest signals of God's intentions for the whole world. The mystical communion of Christians foreshadows the communion of the whole universe of being in the coming kingdom of God. Hope for the church is also hope for the world." (Robert Benne, Roanoke College, Salem, Va., *Ordinary Saints*, page 210)

Our hopes rest not in our commitment but in God's promise. The end of this church's confession points us back to the very beginning, to the Triune God whose inner nature is overflowing in love.

May the ELCA not get stuck in its confession or think that exploring the mysteries of the faith is a substitute for loving service. But may we love our confession of faith so that we are filled with a power beyond our wildest hopes—the power of God to fulfill all that has been promised. To God—Father, Son, and Holy Spirit—be all praise and honor in the church, now and forever.

For reflection

1. The author invites us to explore the mysteries of faith and to live lives of loving spirit. How do you see both these being honored in your congregation?

2. Think of all the "hot topics" and lively questions and challenges facing the church today. In the face of these, what is God's promise?

3. For you, what are the three key "confessions" that support your faith and the faith of the church?

Section Two

Lutheran and Evangelical

Four articles on a variety of themes written between 1988 and 1990.

15

Rebuilding Lutheran Piety

Blueprint for a contemporary Christian faith

This is a good time for American Lutherans to give fresh attention to piety. A great hunger for spiritual experience exists in our society and among our people. But we have been nervous about the possible excesses of emphasizing personal faith, and many Lutheran congregations have been slow to seize this opportunity.

We have allowed other churches—from Roman Catholics to conservative evangelicals—to present themselves as the only ones really interested in shaping spiritual life.

It has not always been so. Three hundred years ago a German Lutheran pastor named Philip Jakob Spener wrote an influential book, *Pia Desideria*. Spener called for a fresh emphasis on Bible study, the priesthood of all Christians, practical Christian service, the reform of preaching and mutual restraint in church controversies. His book sparked great renewal throughout the Lutheran church—with emphasis that influenced John Wesley and the emergence of Methodism in England and America.

This movement, which came to be called pietism, deeply influenced many of the Lutherans who came to America from Europe. At times the movement became dangerously anti-theological and anti-clerical. But at its best it was a powerful tool for renewal.

In recent generations many Lutherans—including some church leaders—have been reacting against the particular piety in which they grew up. They have been eager to leave what seemed to be the narrow, world-denying views of the communities that first nourished them, views that stressed holiness and commitment to Jesus.

Today the danger is not narrow pietism so much as a dry and impersonal form of Christian experience. One pastor even speaks about the dangers of "religion-less Lutheranism." We need themes and disciplines for shaping and strengthening our faith.

Building blocks

There is no one pattern of Christian piety; each denominational tradition has its own special emphases. Nor is there a timeless pattern for piety. The situation of Christians changes from generation to generation. But it is possible to work on a form of Lutheran piety for our time. Piety that does not flee modern life problems or critical thought can be constructed by drawing on some of our theology's rich themes that are appropriate to the struggle to be a Christian today.

This piety would be built from rather traditional materials—not unlike the components that Spener proposed three centuries ago. It should have solid theology behind it, but it should not be abstract or intellectual. Piety, after all, is a readily available form for living as a Christian.

Personal and group Bible study is still key. Lutherans need to see that the Bible is a book for grown-ups, with its deepest themes speaking to issues that could hardly be understood in childhood. We need to come off our fear of being fundamentalist and learn anew a Lutheran evangelical way to be enthusiastic about the Bible.

Knowledge of the catechism takes on a new importance now when many who have entered the church did not have a traditional confirmation experience—or were not very attentive when they did. Knowing the Ten Commandments, the creeds, and the Lord's Prayer is essential. A fresh understanding of sacraments is a very important part of any Lutheran piety today.

Hymns are great shapers of personal faith, and our current worship book provides a wonderful selection of old and new songs of praise and confession. Prayer is central in any Christian piety, but it comes as a surprise to many to discover what St. Paul knew so well—praying is difficult. The Spirit must help us, Paul wrote, "for we do not know how to pray as we ought." Observing the seasons of the church year is also important.

Blueprint for renewal

It is unlikely that a church so large and diverse as the Evangelical Lutheran Church in America can or should foster a single form of piety. There must be legitimate diversity and Christian freedom in the church. But it is possible to name a few themes that could be part of an emphasis throughout the church.

Five key themes hold promise for renewing Lutheran piety. All five have roots in our tradition. They also have a special relevance to the challenge of living as a Christian in the world today. They do not exhaust the possibilities, but they show the kind of emphases that might be possible in worship and preaching, study and small group life.

1. Joy in creation

We live today with a new sense of the earth's fragility. The environmental disasters of recent months have reminded us how great a risk we humans represent to this planet's future. Continuing space probes remind us of the vastness of the universe and sometimes make us feel rather insignificant.

Lutherans ought to have a strong sense of joy in creation and connection with other creatures who depend on God for life. Martin Luther's *Small Catechism* celebrates creation as God's continuing miracle. In this respect creation is in no way canceled by sin—for God is still our creator, still at work ordering life in our world.

We need to recapture that sense of gratitude for life itself as the first of all of God's gifts and the source of religion itself. Many of the best loved hymns in the Lutheran tradition—from *Praise to the Lord, the Almighty* to *Beautiful Savior*—celebrate God's presence in creation in a way that reminds us of our true identity and responsibilities.

2. Recognition of the power of sin and death

Emphasis on sin has certainly been a characteristic Lutheran theme. Some feel Lutherans have overdone this aspect of the faith, leading people to a despair about themselves and human possibility. No doubt such abuses have taken place and perhaps still do.

In our society it is radical to suggest that something is wrong in the world that goes beyond our capacity to fix or improve. Whenever people come to see that "we are in bondage to sin and cannot free ourselves," they are free to hear the gospel as the radical word of grace and deliverance that it really is.

Today this daily acknowledgment of sin needs to be tied more closely to the power and reality of death. Some of us can live for decades during which no one we know dies, leading to dangerous, false assumptions about where our lives are headed.

Ash Wednesday is a key moment in the Lutheran pilgrimage. It powerfully reminds us "that we are dust and to dust we shall return." When we have this awareness daily, our radical dependence on God becomes more evident.

3. God's presence in Jesus Christ

Jesus Christ stands at the heart of any form of Christian piety. But Jesus plays so many roles, meets so many needs, and is conveyed by so many stories and images. What is the heart of what we need to say about Jesus today?

It might be best to first emphasize who Jesus is, not what Jesus does for us. The heart of the Christian message is the good news that God is for us and with us in Jesus Christ. God's presence in our lives is the greatest and most sustaining of all God's gifts.

Much follows from this—themes like the new creation, the forgiveness of sins, the coming kingdom, and our hope in the face of death. But our piety might be stronger and more faithful if we learn to love Jesus not because of what he can do for us or society but for his own sake as God's presence in our lives. Communion has been a very important way in which Christians have learned to draw strength from that presence.

4. Hope for strength and renewal

Today's world seems a mass of problems. The better informed we are, the weaker we may feel about our ability to get through life. The problems seem so great we may wonder if our faith can have any impact on them.

One of piety's key functions is to give us strength for the long haul—to work with great personal problems, to be faithful in relationship and work commitments, to keep caring and working for peace, freedom and justice.

Our Lutheran emphasis on baptism can have an especially helpful role to play at this point. When we remember our baptism rightly, we know that our life is not a natural thing but a gift from God. We then know we are renewed daily by remembering and clinging to God's grace. This identity—centered in Christ and renewed in prayer and meditation—allows us to rise daily to new life rather than throwing up our hands in helplessness.

5. Unity with all people

A special danger for Christians today is the feeling that our faith is merely private or personal. There is a deep and appropriate individual aspect to piety. But good Christian piety also returns us to our neighbors.

Our faith gives us a hopeful way of being linked to all Christians and to all of humanity, loved as it is by God. It protects us against self-pity by reminding us of the terrible struggles that others are experiencing in the Christian community. And the church gives us concrete ways to link our lives and help those in need—whether they are close by or in distant parts of the globe.

Christian piety also links us to the past and to the future. We are protected from living as if our life was the full center of the drama of this world. In our prayers we remember the saints—not only famous Christians but first of all those in our own families and communities who passed the faith on to us. Such prayers link us to the future, to generations yet to come—whether they be our children or not—and to God's gracious intentions for all creation.

Whether these or other themes emerge as central for piety today, what is crucial is that we find a way to work with the spiritual hunger of the people of our churches and communities. Fostering piety is an ongoing Christian task, one that leads us toward active faith and strength for our challenges in the world.

Christian piety gives us the courage and the tools to carry out that simple but very difficult task—speaking with God. Our world is busy with many things. But it is in danger of neglecting that glorious reality which alone can give center and purpose to our lives.

Our church has a strong theology. It needs to work now to deliver that message of grace and hope in a form that can be grasped and applied by those who hunger and thirst for God.

For reflection

1. What is piety? How have you experienced piety or spiritual hunger in your life or in others?

2. The author names a number of basic building blocks for the Christian life. What are these?

3. The author also outlines five themes that can help renew Lutheran piety. Which of these seems to be the most promising starting point in your own yearning for renewal? In your congregation?

16

Ready for Your Lutheran Checkup?

Take the Lutheran literacy quiz

In recent years several popular books have argued that Americans no longer know the basic facts that are the foundation of being well-educated. These books have ignited controversies about what people should know and whether the evidence supports their conclusion of educational deterioration.

The books touched a nerve. And their general direction is confirmed by many studies that show how little Americans know about science, geography, or our country's history. Such evidence suggested to *The Lutheran's* editors that Lutherans might benefit from a checkup of their knowledge of their heritage.

It is difficult to determine whether the members of Evangelical Lutheran Church in America congregations are better or more poorly informed than were Christians in the past. If we know less than we should, it wouldn't be the first time in the church's history.

Martin Luther wrote his catechisms in part because of the terrible ignorance he discovered in the congregations of his region. Many did not even know the Ten Commandments, the Apostles' Creed, or the Lord's Prayer.

The quiz that follows is intended to be a friendly visitor, not a hostile interrogation. It is offered with the hope of motivating ELCA members to enroll in adult education programs in their congregations this year.

Christians today need to work hard to be well-informed. Most believers have busy lives with only a few hours each week for church activities. And the religious pluralism in our society means that there is little reinforcement of Christian faith or even sharing of basic religious information in schools, on television, and in newspapers. To keep our faith lively, we have to be deliberate about our Christian identity and the knowledge that supports it.

Knowing the facts in the quiz below is no sure sign of faith. One may have a great deal of information and still not believe that Jesus Christ is the Son of God or trust in God above all things. And many who may not know these facts have a profound faith to which they are effective witnesses in daily life.

But ignorance is no cause for pride, especially when with a little effort we could better understand the Bible, the history of the church, and our Lutheran heritage. The questions that follow are meant to stretch the mind, to remind you that learning about our faith is a lifelong task and to encourage you to do it.

Part I: The Bible

1. In Genesis 12, God called a man to go to a new land and promised that all nations would bless themselves by him:
    a. Noah
    b. Jacob
    c. Moses
    d. Abraham

2. In Exodus, the Ten Commandments are introduced with a reminder to the people that God had already:
    a. brought them out of Egypt
    b. forgiven their sins
    c. created the world
    d. formed an order of priests

3. Naomi is Ruth's:
    a. sister
    b. mother
    c. mother-in-law
    d. niece

4. Solomon was the son of David and:
    a. Abigail
    b. Bathsheba
    c. Michal
    d. Pharaoh's daughter

5. Elijah the prophet struggled to keep Israel faithful to God against the efforts of those who believed in the god:
    a. Baal
    b. Molech
    c. Zeus
    d. Jupiter

6. "The Lord is my shepherd, I shall not want" is from:
    a. Psalm 1
    b. Psalm 23
    c. Psalm 51
    d. Psalm 119

7. The prophet who was told by God not to say that he was too young:
    a. Matthew
    b. Paul
    c. Moses
    d. Jeremiah

8. In a valley near Jerusalem, Ezekiel saw a vision in which the Lord:
   a. built a highway in the desert
   b. surrounded him with lions
   c. brought dry bones to life
   d. spilled a boiling pot

9. A Gospel with no story of the birth of Jesus is:
   a. Mark
   b. John
   c. both
   d. neither

10. The story in the Gospel of Luke is continued in the book called:
   a. Acts
   b. Hebrews
   c. John
   d. Revelation

11. At the end of Matthew's Gospel, before he is taken up into heaven, Jesus sends the eleven disciples to make disciples and promises:
   a. that his body and blood are given for them
   b. that he will be with them always
   c. that he will build his church on Peter's confession
   d. that they will sit on golden thrones with him

12. In John's Gospel, Jesus wept:
   a. at the unbelief of the Jews
   b. at the beheading of John the Baptist
   c. when he saw his mother at the cross
   d. at the grave of his friend, Lazarus

13. In Acts 8, Philip's explanation of the Scriptures leads to the baptism of a prominent government official from:
    a. Babylon
    b. Ethiopia
    c. India
    d. Rome

14. Paul says in Romans 1 that he is not ashamed:
    a. to work for a living
    b. that Timothy has been circumcised
    c. of the gospel
    d. that Jesus died on the cross

15. "If anyone will not work, let him not eat" is:
    a. a saying of Jesus in the Gospels
    b. a verse in one of the New Testament Epistles
    c. not in the Bible at all

16. Revelation 21 and 22 report that there is no light or lamp needed in the heavenly Jerusalem because:
    a. God is the city's light
    b. all darkness has been driven out
    c. the jewels themselves are so bright
    d. it is lighted by the fire in which evildoers burn

Part II. Church history and Lutheran heritage

17. The canon or list of books that comprise the New Testament was first announced in the year:
    a. A.D. 96
    b. A.D. 367
    c. A.D. 1267
    d. A.D. 1460

18. Christianity became the official religion of the Roman Empire:
    a. after the death of Nero (A.D. 68)
    b. with the conversion of Emperor Constantine (A.D. 325)
    c. after the invasion of Rome by roving tribes (A.D. 476)

19. A reformer who loved nature and called for gospel preaching and simplicity of lifestyles was:
    a. Francis of Assisi
    b. John Calvin
    c. Michelangelo
    d. Melanchthon

20. The person who lived at the same time as Luther was:
    a. Johann Sebastian Bach
    b. Columbus
    c. Karl Marx
    d. Thomas Jefferson

21. In the years before the Reformation, Luther's assignment in the church was:
    a. as a parish priest
    b. lecturing on the Bible
    c. lecturing on law
    d. writing church music

22. Luther favored all of the following except:
    a. government based on biblical models
    b. hospitals to care for the sick in epidemics
    c. public funding of school for both boys and girls
    d. welfare funded from a community treasury

23. Luther's most important theological colleague and author of several of the Lutheran confessions was:
   a. Thomas Aquinas
   b. Augustine
   c. Katherine von Born
   d. Melanchthon

24. John and Charles Wesley founded a reform movement which came to be known as:
   a. Mennonite
   b. Methodist
   c. Moravian
   d. Mormon

25. Henry Melchoir Muhlenberg is best remembered as:
   a. a Christian who enlisted in the Revolutionary Army
   b. the first speaker of the House of Representatives
   c. a Lutheran pastor and church leader in colonial America

26. In the nineteenth century the largest number of Lutheran immigrants came to the United States from:
   a. Norway
   b. Sweden
   c. Finland
   d. Germany

27. During the Civil War, American Lutherans:
   a. divided into Northern and Southern Churches
   b. maintained strict neutrality
   c. were united in their opposition to slavery

28. A social issue that occupied most American Protestant churches deeply in the early years of the twentieth century was:
    a. abortion
    b. homosexuality
    c. mercy killing
    d. prohibition

29. A Lutheran theologian who led the fight against Adolf Hitler and eventually died in a Nazi prison was:
    a. Bonhoeffer
    b. Bultmann
    c. Kierkegaard
    d. Schweitzer

30. Today one would find a large Lutheran church in all of the following except:
    a. Algeria
    b. Brazil
    c. Namibia
    d. Papua New Guinea

31. The American Lutheran Church and Lutheran Church in America first began to ordain women in:
    a. 1930
    b. 1962
    c. 1970
    d. 1981

32. The Augsburg Confession teaches that we "receive forgiveness of sin and become righteous before God":
- a. by faith
- b. by grace
- c. for Christ's sake
- d. all of these

33. Luther's *Small Catechism* teaches that water in baptism "can produce such great effects" because:
- a. water is a symbol of life
- b. John baptized Jesus
- c. God's word is connected to the water
- d. God is all powerful

34. In the Lord's Supper, Christ's presence comes:
- a. only to those who receive Christ in faith
- b. only to those who believe what the creeds teach
- c. only to those who have prepared by true confession
- d. to all, but unbelievers received judgment, not blessing

35. In terms of human freedom, Lutherans teach that:
- a. freedom was destroyed in the fall of Adam and Eve
- b. freedom was restored to all in the death of Christ
- c. freedom is an inalienable right from our Creator
- d. humans are free in some things, not free in others

36. "I believe that by my own reason or strength I cannot believe in Jesus Christ my Lord, or come to him" is:
- a. a statement by Paul in the Epistle to the Romans
- b. a statement by Luther in the *Small Catechism*
- c. a part of the prayer before communion
- d. none of the above

37. The "two kingdoms" doctrine for Lutherans refers to:
    a. the differing ways God works in the church and the world
    b. the separation of church and state in modern times
    c. the division of Germany into East and West

See answers on page 78.

For reflection

1. After taking and scoring your answers to the literacy quiz, in which area were you most surprised by the correct answers?
2. Are there aspects of this quiz that you'd like to explore more with others? How could you do that in your congregation?

17

Lutheran Thinkers: What's It All about, Martin?

The roles of theologians in the ELCA

Church bodies are held together by many kinds of glue. Some have common family or ethnic ties. Others have a unique structure or organization. Most provide a predictable form of worship—formal or informal—that allows people to move from one congregation to another. Many churches find their unity in strong, visible leaders or in a common mission program. All churches have commonly accepted beliefs or teachings.

While Lutherans have used all the forms of glue available in the American context, they have viewed theology as the key unifying factor. Differences about basic beliefs divided American Lutherans in the past and divide some today. But all agree theology is crucial.

Lutherans have looked to Scripture, the creeds, and their confessions not only as past documents, but as present guides for the life and mission of the church. Little wonder then that theologians have played an important role in the history of the Lutheran church. For the most part this role has been informal, in contrast to the teaching authority of bishops in some other traditions. But theologians have exercised great influence through training pastors, writing and speaking for the church and serving as mediators in periods of division and uncertainty.

At times they have been honored and expected, but at other times resented for their tendency to press critical questions and speak against inadequate compromise.

Lutherans have not always understood the theologians' dilemma. He or she loves the church, cares about it passionately, and wants to speak well of it. On the other hand, the theologian has been entrusted a critical task—testing current teaching and church practices to see if they are faithful to that gospel received in Scripture and the Lutheran confessions. The theologian sometimes must be sharply critical to get the attention of a busy church that wants to "get on with the work."

Who are the people who will be the theologians for the Evangelical Lutheran Church in America? On the one hand, the theological task of being faithful and speaking imaginatively to our time belongs to the whole people of God. On the other hand, pastors and other church workers have a special responsibility, and seminaries work to help future pastors see themselves as parish theologians.

But the roster of working theologians tends to include those who have graduate training which equips them for ministries of teaching and leadership in the church. Perhaps most of the theologians teach in the church's seminaries, although a number of distinguished ones teach at ecumenical, university-based divinity schools.

Theologians also may be found in college teaching, parish ministry, among the bishops, and working for church agencies. The ELCA Division for Ministry is charged to "provide for a regular and representative convocation of theologians involved in the teaching ministry of this church." They face a dilemma knowing just who should be invited.

The matter is further complicated by the variety of disciplines in which theologians work. Some work in Old and New Testament, others in church history, systematic theology—best understood as the teachings of the church today—or in ethics. Still others work in the disciplines of practical theology—liturgy, Christian education, pastoral care, preaching, church and community, administration, mission, stewardship, and evangelism.

In the past, most theologians have been ordained pastors and, given Lutheran history, have been white males. Today this is changing as women and people of color have emerged as important theological thinkers. Also, there are an increasing number of lay Lutheran theologians such as Robert Benne, Elizabeth Bettenhausen, Faith Burgess, Gracia Grindal, Mary Hughes, George Lindbeck, Michael Root, and Martha Stortz.

To many in the church, few things are more puzzling than the theologians' disagreements with each other. Aside from differences of training and temperament, Lutheran theologians divide around a couple of basic issues.

The first involves the task of theology itself. One group sees their task as conserving the faith and presenting it with vigor to a new generation. They are not all conservatives, but theologians of this type do give the inherited Christian tradition the benefit of the doubt. They are aware that Lutherans in America have a hard time holding on to their distinctive heritage in the midst of the wide variety of religious opinions and general indifference to theology in the United States.

A second group sees dialogue with the modern world as the theological task for today. These theologians are not indifferent to tradition, but most of their energy is spent trying to see how the church can understand and learn from modern philosophy, sociology, and the arts. They fear Lutherans may hide behind their heritage and fail to be in mission to a world much changed since the first or sixteenth century.

A third group—perhaps a variation of the second—recently has emerged. These theologians center their work on questions stemming from suffering and injustice in today's world. They fear theology can be a way to protect the church from working for change and justice in a troubled world. These Lutheran theologians are strongly influenced by the various stands of liberation theology—Latin American, black, and feminist, for example.

Most theologians try to balance concern for the tradition, dialogue with contemporary society, and the concern for justice which stems from the gospel. But they differ on how much priority should be given each item.

Their views of the ecumenical movement also differ. Many are deeply impressed with the results of twenty years of dialogue with the Roman Catholic Church and hope Lutherans will pursue better relations here—as long as it may take—in order that the original division of the Reformation might be overcome.

Some of these theologians are especially happy with the current "interim Eucharistic sharing" between Lutherans and Episcopalians and believe it will help both those churches in their dialogues with Roman Catholics. Others, however, are suspicious of what they call a "tilt toward Rome." They urge Lutherans to assert their identity as Protestants and move closer to churches with Reformation traditions. Still others urge caution about any specific ecumenical direction until deep understanding has been reached that can be the basis for lasting agreement.

One thing is clear: American Lutheran theologians are too diverse to tilt the church in any one particular direction. Their positions reflect differences that exist within the Lutheran churches. But they seem virtually united in some concerns:

- The erosion of Lutheran teaching, especially at the level of catechetical instruction.
- The importance of serious reflection on ecumenical dialogue.
- The need to find a way to work for injustice that fits with Lutheran confessional theology.
- The quality of seminary education today.

How could the ELCA best make use of its theologians? Three things would be helpful:

1. Use theologians to help study difficult issues, but invite them before conclusions have been reached.
The new church faces many difficult issues—from the understanding of ministry, to baptism and confirmation, future ecumenical

> ### A warning to the theologians
> *Martin Luther, deeply aware of the temptations of taking oneself too seriously—an occupational hazard for theologians—offered this warning to fellow theologians in 1539:*
>
> If, however, you feel and are inclined to think you have made it, flattering yourself with your own little books, teaching, or writing, because you have done it beautifully and preached excellently; if you are highly pleased when someone praises you in the presence of others; if you perhaps look for praise, and would sulk or quit what you are doing if you did not get it—if you are of that stripe, dear friend, then take yourself by the ears, and if you do this in the right way you will find a beautiful pair of big, long, shaggy donkey ears. Then do not spare any expense! Decorate them with golden bells, so that people will be able to hear you wherever you go, point their fingers at you and say, "See, See! There goes that clever beast, who can write such exquisite books and preach so remarkably well." (Martin Luther, "Preface to the Wittenberg Edition of Luther's German Writings" [1539] in *Luther's Works,* Volume 34, pages 287-88)

direction, and divisive social questions like abortion or policy toward Central America. Theologians have expertise and training to offer as these issues are studied. Their gifts need to be complimented by other voices from the church.

A deep complaint of many theologians involves the church's tendency to bring them into a study process late to pronounce a theological blessing on a decision virtually decided, or to write a theological rationale for a decision made on other grounds.

2. Invite theologians to address the church in its assemblies, but do not expect them to provide entertainment.

Lutheran theologians with a wide variety of views increasingly are invited to address conventions, clergy and lay convocations, and other church meetings. This is something most theologians find a joy and a privilege.

But because the church tends not to understand the critical side of the theological task, some are surprised when a theologian criticizes church practice or is less than entertaining. Theologians have failings of, at times, being quarrelsome or even boring. But the church needs to respect the freedom of the theologian to ask the hard and necessary question: "Are we doing and saying what we ought to do and say?"

3. Take their suggestions for the church's life seriously, but invite the whole church to debate what they propose.

Theologians become rather impressed with their own importance. (See the warning to them from fellow theologian Martin Luther on page 66.) They do not expect everyone to agree with their suggestions, nor even to like them, especially when their remarks are intended to shake up a sleepy church and to move it to think.

But Lutherans owe it to their theologians to take their ideas and suggestions seriously enough to read them, listen to them, and discuss them. If theology is to be glue which can hold the ELCA together, the voices of theologians will have to be heard. They have a service to perform—the necessary but difficult task of holding the church to the beliefs it claims to treasure.

Voices of the theologians

Black Lutheran theologians from Africa and North America:
. . . Justification and justice must never be separated, for God's will for humanity is justice. In consequence, those who have God's mercy in Christ are called to seek after, work for, and engage themselves in those activities that will bring about justice for those who are oppressed. (*A message from Harare by Black Lutherans*, page 3)

Carl Braaten, professor of systematic theology, Lutheran School of Theology in Chicago:
Some of us have said this so often that it hardly bears repeating: Lutheranism is not essentially a church but a movement. It is not essentially an independent church in competition with other denominational churches. It is a confessional movement that exists for the sake of reforming the whole church of Christ by the canon of the gospel. The ecclesiastical, organizational structures of Lutheranism are interim measures, ready to go out of business as soon as their provisional aims are realized. (*Principles of Lutheran Theology*, page 46)

Gerhard Forde, professor of systematic theology, Luther-Northwestern Seminary, St. Paul, Minn.:
Justification by faith always appears dangerous, because of our incurable tendency to think in terms of law, virtue, and moral progress. Church people, religious people, and their teachers are especially inclined to think that way. Hence justification by faith generally has most difficulty precisely in the church. (Carl Braaten and Robert Jenson editors, *Christian Dogmatics, II*, page 409)

Robert Jenson, professor of systematic theology, Lutheran Seminary at Gettysburg, Penn.:
Whatever group is to ponder matters vital in the church must be allowed, and indeed compelled, actually to deliberate, to think together, to track down the problem and create a solution. A mere head count, even one taken at a meeting after positions have been stated, is not the way in which sovereign decisions may be made in the church. ("Sovereignty in the Church" in *The New Church Debate*, page 49)

George Lindbeck, Pitkin Professor of Historical Theology, Yale Divinity School, New Haven, Conn.:
In the present situation, . . . the churches primarily accommodate to the prevailing culture rather than shape it. . . . They continue to embrace in one way or another the majority of the population and must cater willy-nilly to majority trends. This makes it difficult for them to attract assiduous catechumens even

from among their own children, and when they do, they generally prove wholly incapable of providing effective instruction in distinctively Christian language and practice. (*The Nature of Doctrine*, page 133)

Mary Pellauer, director of studies, ELCA Commission for Women, Chicago:
Feminist theology does not live from any specific denominational heritage. The tensions and problems, both practical and theological, experienced by women in the churches are similar across institutional lines. Few feminists would speak of any denominational theology in the way that we Lutherans speak of "Lutheran theology" with such ease and familiarity. Our community of accountability is not constrained by the denominational lines that men have drawn. ("Feminist Theology: Challenges and Consolations for Lutherans" in *Dialog*, Volume 24.1, page 20)

Lee Snook, professor of systematic theology, Luther-Northwestern Seminary, St. Paul, Minn.:
(The) long history of the church's use of Scripture is also a history of biases, a fact which recent historians have called to our attention by uncovering the way certain interpretations of the Jesus story have protected, reinforced, and sanctioned anti-Semitism, sexism, and social elitism within the church. Only by revising the prevailing interpretations of Jesus can the hurt inflicted upon Jews, women, Blacks, and others be reduced. (*The Anonymous Christ*, page 25)

For reflection

1. The author describes three groups of theologians. Which group has the most appeal for you? Are there any that you had never heard of before?

2. What topics would you like a theologian to explore at your next synod assembly? Why are these crucial questions today?

3. How could teaching theologians work more closely with parish theologians and leaders of congregations?

18

The Gospel Truth about Being Evangelical

Lutherans need to re-examine this old family term that others define too narrowly

When I was a boy, I belonged to St. John Church in Fremont, Ohio. From time to time I noted that the real name of the congregation was longer and more complicated: St. John *Evangelical* Lutheran Church. On the cornerstone and in church bulletins on special occasions the formal name was used.

I wondered about this and asked my father. He told me that we were, in fact, an *evangelical* church. I asked what the word meant. He explained that we were a church devoted to the Gospel.

Still I was confused. Shouldn't all churches want to be devoted to the Gospel, live by the Gospel, and share the Gospel with all people? Were all churches evangelical, I wondered, or just Lutherans?

Today we hear much about evangelicals. People are understandably confused, especially in Lutheran churches. Lutherans have no copyright on the term. A major movement within the Church of England is called evangelicalism. A church in the United States and Canada, now part of the United Church of Christ, was once called Evangelical and Reformed. Then there are the conservative evangelicals such as the Southern Baptists, the Pentecostals, and the Holiness groups, considered to be a strong force in American religious life today.

All this is confusing enough to drive churches to erase the word from their constitutions and cornerstones. But the name "evangelical" is an essential part of Lutheran identity. It all goes back to a Greek word *euangelion*, meaning "the good news of the Christian message." The word refers to a surprising and hopeful message:

70

Now after John was arrested, Jesus came into Galilee, preaching the Gospel of God, and saying, "The time is fulfilled, and the kingdom of God is at hand; repent, and believe in the Gospel" (Mark 1:14-15).

Such good news is found not only in the four Gospels, but also throughout the New Testament. When properly interpreted it can be found at many other places in the Bible as well.

Obviously Lutherans do not have a corner on the good news of salvation which God announced and accomplished in Jesus Christ. But the Gospel as *the evangelical principle* does play a special role in the life and teaching of our church, at least when we are faithful to our own confessions.

What does it mean to a Lutheran Christian to be called *evangelical?* It means several different, important things.

An evangelical Christian uses the Gospel as the key to interpreting Scripture. Of course all churches use the Bible in some way and with some seriousness. Lutherans would never dare to claim that theirs is the only church that takes the Bible seriously. Rather, the Lutheran church knows that the Bible is difficult to interpret. How can we understand what we read unless we have some clue to the theme, the unity, the basic message of this large and confusing book?

We are truly evangelical when we use the Gospel as that key to unlock the mystery of the meaning of Scripture. All of it is God's word, all of it is written to be "profitable for teaching, for reproof, for correction, and for training in righteousness" (2 Timothy 3:16). But the heart of the message is the good news that Jesus came, preaching the news of salvation, freely offered to those who believe.

Lutherans know and affirm that they belong to a Bible-centered church, one which is rooted in God's word as humanity's hope and constant guide. But evangelical Lutherans go even further to declare that the heart of the Bible is the joyful good news that God has loved us and come to us.

An evangelical Christian receives and accepts the Gospel as it is expressed in word and sacrament. The Gospel is not just information. Paul thanks God that at Thessalonica "our Gospel came to you not only in word, but also in power and in the Holy Spirit and with full conviction" (1 Thessalonians 1:5). We are renewed in the Gospel and empowered to live in its assurance of God's grace and love not only through sermons and Bible reading, but also through baptism and communion.

The evangelical Lutheran church will differ from some others that call themselves evangelical. Others emphasize the Bible, and we agree on its importance. But Lutherans teach that the same Gospel comes to us when a person is baptized, when a sermon is preached, when the community shares the body and blood of Christ.

God is present with us and for us in other ways too—in prayer, in common life, in various rites and occasions. But our understanding of the Gospel is such that we don't have to go out and search for God. God has searched for *us* and comes to us in reliable and predictable ways. We strive in our church life to see that each of these means of grace receives its appropriate attention.

An evangelical Christian knows that the spirit of the Gospel is freedom. This is the lesson hammered out in the epistle to the Galatians. The lesson must be learned anew in each Christian generation. "For freedom Christ has set us free; stand fast therefore, and do not submit again to a yoke of slavery." Paul teaches this with clarity but it is a feature of the good news throughout Scripture.

Freedom is a painful thing for human beings to accept. We dream of being free, but when confronted with God's great gift of freedom in the Gospel, we feel anxiety. We want someone to give us clear answers, to tell us what to do, to make the world more predictable. In Jesus God has not given us what we want, but what we need—the true freedom for which we were created.

This is a key test question whenever we are confused about whether some new movement or personality is evangelical in the deepest sense. We need to listen carefully to see whether this spirit of freedom in Christ is present in what is being presented. There is a place for law in the life of a Christian, but those who know the good news of what God has done in Jesus Christ also know that freedom must be the style of our new life in Christ.

An evangelical Christian knows that the Gospel is offered to all people, and that the church must therefore be an inclusive community. This was one of the most difficult lessons for the Christian community whose history we read in the book of Acts. Early Christians could not imagine that God really intended to create a new people that would include Jews and Gentiles, men and women, slaves and free people within the same movement. But the church isn't a human community. The church is the creation of the Holy Spirit who is always expanding our horizons to recognize new brothers and sisters in Christ.

This too is an excellent test question for so-called evangelical movements in our time. Racial and sexual equality in our society has been difficult for many to accept. Legitimate differences exist within the church about strategy and tactics for achieving these goals. But a church that is centered in the Gospel can never be turned inward or toward the past, comfortable with a parish where everyone is like-minded. The word which is good news for us also is a source of stirring and urgency to reach out to share this same good news with others, even across deep differences.

The Lutheran Confessions contain a long description of other implications of making the Gospel central for a truly evangelical church. One of the most important is the sense that we are not yet perfect, that we have not yet arrived at the fullness of the promises of God, and that we cannot arrive at such a point by our own striving.

This point too is bitterly debated in our time. Some preach and teach as if perfection were possible in this life. Some speak as if it were possible to know true Christians by their behavior, their piety, their attitude on social issues. But the spirit of the Gospel warns again and again against being content with one's own righteousness.

Augustine saw so clearly that even Christian saints have a need to pray daily, "Forgive us our sins." This means that there cannot be any sense of smugness or pride within the church as to how good we are and how wicked the world is. Our freedom does not include the possibility of proclaiming ourselves the moral majority, the righteous remnant, those who really are faithful to God. If we want to boast, then as Paul said so long ago, it will not be in ourselves (1 Corinthians 1:28-29).

A Lutheran wants to be known as an evangelical, even at the risk of being misunderstood. We cannot abandon that important name for ourselves simply because others (with whom we partially disagree) have been using the term. In important ways we can learn from them what we may have forgotten about our own heritage. Even disagreements, in love, can be a source of new life and renewal for us.

But what about the term "conservative-evangelical"? Many Lutherans have been asked whether they are conservative-evangelicals. They might well answer *yes* by the following logic:

- I do think of myself as conservative.
- I have been taught that the church—our church—is evangelical.
- Therefore, I must be one of these much-discussed conservative-evangelicals.

Certainly a Lutheran Christian may be both conservative and evangelical. Perhaps the majority of Lutherans in the past five centuries have been. But putting the terms together has unfortunate implications.

In the realm of politics the Lutheran church would not be identified with any particular ideology—either liberal or conservative. The church is in great danger when it surrenders its freedom in the Gospel to a particular political stand. We have hoped, as Lutherans, not to be a small sect or movement within society but to be an open and inclusive church in which different sorts of people can come together around their common need for and response to the Gospel. A "conservative church" or a "liberal church" cripples its outreach from the start.

This does not mean that the church should be remote from the issues of the world or neutral or middle-of-the-road in the controversies of the day. The church should in some deep sense be *both* liberal and conservative. If conservatism implies holding for lasting and substantial values against the fads and trends that shake each generation, then the church is rightly conservative. If liberal implies a commitment to justice in society and a special concern for those who are in need, then liberalism will follow inevitably from the Gospel.

But none of this translates into a neat political program. The Lutheran Church in America has been struggling to overcome the typical Lutheran pattern in church history of indifference to injustice and automatic alliance with the status quo. The LCA social statements of the last twenty years have been an exciting new development, a sign of a church's determination to wrestle with the issues of the world in which it is called to proclaim the Gospel.

The Gospel is not just an inner and private relationship between a person and God. The Gospel is a word of power and life, with hopeful implications for *this life* and for *this world* as well as an even deeper hope for the life to come. The church ought to surprise us, even as the Gospel does, sometimes being liberal over against our stubborn comfort with the status quo, at other times being staunchly and rightly conservative over against our optimism that there are simple solutions to the deep problems of how we live together in this world.

The glorious Gospel, which transcends and unites even the sharpest conservative—liberal conflicts—should never be used to rally converts or allies to one program or the other. We object to *conservative-evangelical* just as we must continue to object to *liberal-evangelical.* The Gospel is in a class by itself and cannot be successfully crossed with any merely human options, however fine, however noble.

Liberals and conservatives alike charge that those who differ from themselves do not really deserve the name *evangelical.* All might do well to take a closer look at those who seem to be the problem in the church today.

Those disgusted and impatient with the stirring of conservative-evangelicals and Pentecostals should look closely at the life of the Lutheran church to see whether everything is really in order. Renewal—including renewal of spirit, of commitment, of knowledge of the Bible and perhaps even of piety—is greatly needed today. We are always in danger of becoming a church so inclusive and so flexible that the Gospel becomes a limp and nebulous center rather than a word of power and life and freedom.

Those disgusted and impatient with the seeming inertia of a Lutheran church that claims to be evangelical should look at the institution to see whether it is quite as hopeless as it seems. Our social statements may be a sign of being shaped by the society at large. But they may also be a sign of a church that has finally learned to see the implications of the Gospel for daily life. Our ecumenical activity could spring from a sense that there is no real difference among Christian groups. But it may spring from a sense that those differences are different—and less dividing—than we had supposed.

Yes, call me evangelical—even at the risk of being misunderstood. To do so will get a good discussion started about what the Gospel is and about what is important in the mission of the church. But do not call me conservative-evangelical or liberal-evangelical. The miracle of the church has always been that the Holy Spirit is able to bring people together, even across barriers as deep as those formidable political labels.

For reflection

1. When you hear the word *evangelical* what images come to mind? How well do those images match the understanding presented here?

2. The author names four marks of evangelical identity for Lutherans—emphasis on the Gospel, Word and Sacrament, freedom, and inclusive community. Which do you find the most surprising?

3. What are the signs that the congregation to which you belong is *evangelical?* How would you explain that evangelical identity to friends who are not Lutheran?

Answers

Part I

1. **D**   2. **A**   3. **C**   4. **B**   5. **A**   6. **B**   7. **D**   8. **C**   9. **C**   10. **A**
11. **B**   12. **D**   13. **B**   14. **C**   15. **B**   16. **A**

Part II

17. **B**   18. **B**   19. **A**   20. **B**   21. **B**   22. **A**   23. **D**   24. **B**   25. **C**
26. **D**   27. **A**   28. **D**   29. **A**   30. **A**   31. **C**   32. **D**   33. **C**
34. **D**   35. **D**   36. **B**   37. **A**

Scoring

28-37 You don't need encouragement; you ought to be teaching.

18-27 You haven't been asleep, but there's more to learn.

10-17 Of course you're busy, but you could find some time.

0-9 You're still welcome, even with a lot to learn.

Section Three

The ELCA at Five

Two articles in which Lull looks at early accomplishments of the ELCA and outlines reasons for hope for the church's future.

19

Reason to Believe

The gospel is lived among us, and we know the church's future is secure with God

"Are you hopeful about our church?" people ask me as I speak in various parts of the country. Few of them regret the merger. I sense they want to be optimistic. But few are excited about the ELCA, or even yet accustomed to the new name, new priorities, and new ways of doing things.

These mixed feelings make Lutherans like members of other American church bodies. Presbyterians, Methodists, and Episcopalians have discontentments with their denominations. Even historically strong churches like the Southern Baptist Convention or Roman Catholic Church show many signs of disagreement.

But Evangelical Lutheran Church in America members have reasons to be optimistic. Recent achievements of Lutheran churches are quite remarkable. In the years since 1960, the churches that came together to form the ELCA made exciting changes:

They continued to build new congregations as members moved to new parts of the United States, especially to the Sun Belt where there were few Lutheran churches.

They learned to make social statements on pressing problems. Overcoming the Lutheran tendency to avoid social issues, they used their heritage as the theological basis for such social witness.

They entered into the great wave of ecumenical dialogue, setting aside Lutheran hesitations about ecumenism. They discovered new levels of understanding with old opponents even on traditionally difficult questions like the nature of the Lord's Supper.

They worked at renewing worship, recovering much of their Lutheran heritage and discovering new possibilities with the *Lutheran Book of Worship.*

They voted to ordain women in 1970, carrying out this change with surprisingly little formal opposition.

Hope-filled signs

Any church that accomplished these major gains in the last generation has every reason to hope that it is still a vital community that can resolve new challenges.

I am hopeful for the ELCA because I see many signs of vitality, especially in congregations and synods. And this, after all, is where most of us can invest ourselves with the hope of making a difference.

I also sense a growing forbearance on the part of many church leaders, activists, critics, and theologians. This church began its life filled with people holding strong—and conflicting—agendas for what should be taught, for social witness and for program direction.

Our bishops and church executives are relearning the need to build consensus, to pay the bills, and to make the case for the institution and its mission. Many activists now see the need to build coalitions and bring people along. Perhaps even theologians are learning that while their critique of the church is necessary, a positive tone and a persuasive spirit are as important as correct arguments and a loud voice.

We still have potentially explosive commitments among us. But most ELCA members seem eager not to blow the church apart on social issues (abortion, sexuality), ecumenical direction (where people have quite contradictory hopes), or on questions of how we order ministry and do evangelism. On a number of fronts, the ELCA has sought a third way, between extreme positions, even on issues as socially polarized as abortion.

This forbearance, a fine biblical virtue, can turn to cowardice if we avoid important issues out of fear. But it can adorn the church if it means taking time to listen and to develop a position that can be widely supported with some enthusiasm.

Such churchly self-restraint is more than a way to hold a church together. It may help us remember our special vocation as a church that clings to Martin Luther's concept of Christian freedom, emphasizing both freedom and responsibility. If we cling to this, we will not feel that to be strong a church must be bossy, domineering, and instructing its members what to do or not to do in every aspect of life. On the other hand, we will call people to responsibility, illumine important issues, and offer general principles for personal conduct and our common life.

We need more joy

But if we have reasons to be hopeful, we also have continuing reasons for concern.

Highly committed people work in the ELCA's churchwide structure. But many members still see a gap between "Higgins Road" and the struggles of congregations, many of whom feel neither understood nor cared about.

Election quotas continue to trouble some Lutherans. This is chiefly because the positive, mission-based argument for guaranteeing diverse voices in leadership still has not been clearly explained at the grass-roots level.

The ELCA has suffered financial problems for complex reasons, including rising healthcare costs for church workers. Seminaries, church colleges, campus and urban ministries have especially suffered as their grants have been cut.

But what perplexes me most about the ELCA these days is how little joy Lutherans seem to have about being Lutheran. We Lutherans generally have been admired for our ability to preach the gospel with power, for informed sacramental worship, for our deep theology of the cross, and for our passion for teaching, especially the young.

These strengths seem hidden. These days we often are gloomy, more weighed down with problems of self-justification as a church than full of grace-centered self-confidence.

Before its birth there were battles about the ELCA's structure. Since then another set of battles has followed: ecumenical direction, deacons and bishops, quotas, gay and lesbian ordination, sexuality studies, what to do with the seminaries.

These have left us too little time to rediscover what we have in common with each other. Although many of us have begun to find new friends in the ELCA during its early years, we still have not quite succeeded in discovering that we share a deep faith that has life-transforming power. This discovery can renew our church, open us to mission and move us to like—and, in time, to love—one another in this church.

What next?

Looking to the ELCA's next five years, for what might we hope? If our nation is truly entering a time of greater national consensus to solve problems, that will spill over to our church. The society in which we live shapes our life in the church far more than we usually acknowledge.

But one negative effect of living in this society is that we receive very little positive support for being Christians. Our families and congregations are giving off warning signs that we have neglected the basics—Bible, catechism, Christian ethics. Our people are generally not well-informed about what it means to be a Lutheran Christian. Some have left for other churches because of a spiritual hunger we seemed unready or unable to meet. That is why:

The ELCA must become a teaching church again. If it is not, we will not have any common language to tie us together, any basis for resolving our differences other than political preferences, any vision that lifts us beyond what we are.

Our church needs to more deeply reflect the concerns of laity. Average church members care far less about social statements or restructuring our ministry than about the pain in their families, job stress, violence, and the fear that the church is sometimes too rigid and other times too quick to change.

In his recent book, *Protestants,* Harvard historian Stephen Ozment argued that the Reformation was a success, in part, because its leaders understood and acted upon church members' long-term frustrations. Today we need to do such listening and then rearrange our priorities if our church is to make an impact beyond our own churchly structures and meetings.

We need to engage in a decade of experimentation. The signs of forbearance among us suggest we might be able to trust one another to do this—in liturgy, evangelism, teaching, and parish structure for ministry—without making everything the same in all parts of the country or having everything approved by the central office. Genuine renewal for mission can happen when we Lutherans lighten up and back off on some of our harsh judgments, our need to control and our anxiety about those Lutherans who aren't exactly like us.

The Spirit has called us to live in this big church with many who are very different from ourselves and with less continuity with our past than many of us would like. It's a hard journey.

But we can find refreshment by having some fun being Lutherans. Let's laugh at ourselves, not only because we can be so serious and so silly but because the gospel is loved among us and because we know that our church's future is secure with God.

As we rediscover this deepest of all truths, we will become hopeful knowing the Spirit continues to work, even in our 5-year-old church, even in mildly discouraging times.

For reflection

1. Writing in 1993, Dr. Lull describes some of the achievements of the Lutherans in America from 1960-1990. What would you name as the most noteworthy accomplishments of the ELCA since its formation in 1988?

2. Describe in your own words what is meant by "a third way"? Does that fit with your experiences in the ELCA?

3. The author lists three challenges for the ELCA: to become a teaching church again, to reflect more deeply the concerns of laity, and to engage in a decade of experimentation in liturgy, evangelism, teaching, and parish structure. From your perspective, how well has the ELCA honored those challenges?

4. Write a letter to be read by church leaders in 2010. What challenges do you set before the church to which you belong?

20

Ten Signs of Hope

Changes in the 20th century should encourage us for the 21st

What will become of our church? As we enter a new century—and even a new millennium—North American Lutherans are wondering about the prospects for their church. A few are hopeful. Many more are skeptical or pessimistic. But if the achievements of the past one hundred years offer any clues, we ought to be encouraged about the future.

In at least ten ways, the twentieth century transformed the churches that united to form the ELCA. By surveying the entire list, you begin to see the Spirit's work in our repeated ability to meet new challenges.

1. From many churches to the ELCA

We were divided one hundred years ago into dozens of church bodies, distinguished by language, piety, and church organization. Lutheran leaders worked throughout the century to unite into a stronger, more effective church. Not all have come together yet, and the ELCA may not be the last chapter in this history. But it's a remarkable achievement that we shouldn't take for granted.

2. From pastoral domination to shared leadership

Highly educated Lutheran pastors, most of them immigrants, were the dominant figures in congregations one hundred years ago. We haven't achieved a complete flowering of the priesthood of all the baptized, but we have found ways to share leadership in our congregations.

This is a real strength. Clergy and laity need to work together to meet local mission challenges of the next century.

3. From quietism to social action

The great wars of the twentieth century and a growing sense of injustice in our society and world have taught the necessity to speak about the great issues of our time—racism, war and peace, economic justice, medical ethics. We don't have complete agreement about what to say, but most have come to accept that our church must speak to what is happening in our world.

4. From theology importers to leadership

Lutheran theology in 1900 was largely imported from Europe. But American Lutherans found their voice and now write works that are studied by Lutherans and more broadly. Since mid-century, distinguished voices such as Joseph Sittler, Arthur Karl Piepkorn, Martin Marty, George Forell, George Lindbeck, William Lazareth, and a host of others have given U.S. Lutherans a respected voice.

5. From sermon-centered to word-and-sacrament congregations

The twentieth century has brought a series of hymnals that help Lutherans recover lost parts of their Reformation heritage, especially the centrality of baptism and communion.

Lutherans also learned to sing hymns from many other traditions and are learning songs from all parts of the world. Local study groups around the new common lectionary help pastors maintain a disciplined approach to God's word, which alone gives life to the church.

6. From colonists to global partners

Throughout the twentieth century Lutherans have had a strong interest in global missions. But the end of colonialism after World War I brought deeper awareness of the ambiguity of mission and the question of how to separate sharing the Christian gospel from the exporting of American culture.

With the ELCA Companion Synod program, a new generation is being recruited to enthusiasm about world Christianity and the vital Lutheran presence within it.

7. From North and East to South and West

American Lutherans in 1900 were concentrated in a belt that ran from Pennsylvania to Montana. Pockets of Lutherans existed in the Carolinas, Texas, and in the Pacific Northwest. But Lutherans were strongly present only in the East and the Midwest.

The great mobility after World War II challenged the church to organize thousands of congregations in places such as Florida, Arizona, and California. Today, Lutheran congregations are present in every part of the country.

8. From struggling to strong church institutions

In the nineteenth century, Lutherans began to build colleges, seminaries, and institutions for the needy. Their twentieth-century children and grandchildren continued to build a formidable network of colleges, seminaries, social service agencies, camps, and campus ministries that provide much of our church's connective reality. Many people who can't define a "synod" have a strong loyalty to these ministries.

9. From men only to the ordination of women

Perhaps no development would surprise our forebears more than the ordination of women in 1970. This was possible because of good theological leadership and the presence of highly credible women. Effects of this change continue to unfold, but I consider it one of the great blessings of the past fifty years.

Hard times and disappointments

The 20th century has not seen progress in every area for American Lutherans.

The period of World War I was a time of prejudice, discrimination, and violence toward many U.S. Lutherans, who were put out of homes, jobs, and churches because of their ethnic heritage.

Mid-century hopes for a merger of most U.S. Lutherans, including the Lutheran Church-Missouri Synod, weren't fulfilled.

Lutherans have lost ground in some areas. One of these is parish education. While excellent exceptions exist, most congregations don't have strong enough teaching programs to prepare members for discipleship in a world that is largely indifferent to faith.

The opportunities of the media revolution—film and television—have not yet been seized. Our church has only recently begun to explore these, which accounts for our marginal presence in this vital area that shapes our culture.

Lutherans have only tentatively embraced multicultural outreach as a major priority and God-given opportunity for renewal. I hope a future historian might list it among the accomplishments of our time.

—Timothy F. Lull

10. From isolation to ecumenical leadership

American Lutherans in the nineteenth century worked hard not to lose their identity in the melting pot of Protestant America. In 1900 most practiced "close" communion and did so until after World War II. But during the last fifty years Lutherans have shown great leadership in ecumenical dialogue and bilateral agreements.

The ELCA established full communion with the Presbyterians, the Reformed Church in America, the United Church of Christ, and the Moravians and have proposed an accord with the Episcopal Church. U.S. Lutherans were also influential in the theological work toward the *Joint Declaration on the Doctrine of Justification* with the Roman Catholic Church (see page 40).

Reviewing what God has done with and through Lutherans in the twentieth century, I can't be discouraged about the challenges confronting the church.

People of faith can never be pessimistic, however great the challenges. The *Augsburg Confession* got it right in 1530: "It is also taught among us that one holy Christian church will be and remain forever."

This doesn't promise an expanded Lutheran market share in U.S. religious life. But it points to our always-generous God in whose name the future is always full of promise.

Timeline

1966: Inter-Lutheran Commission for Worship forms to plan for a new worship book.

1967: Lutheran-Episcopal dialogue begins.

1967: The National Lutheran Council is re-formed as the Lutheran Council in the U.S.A. by the ALC, the LCA, and the LCMS.

1969: LCMS elects J. A. O. Preus as president and approves altar-and-pulpit-fellowship with the ALC.

1970: ALC and LCA recommendation to separate confirmation and first communion, allowing children to commune at earlier ages.

1970: Elizabeth Platz is the first female Lutheran pastor in North America.

1970: ALC adopts provisional use of the title bishop.

1973: LCMS moderates form Evangelical Lutherans in Mission in response to actions of the LCMS convention.

1974: Students, faculty, and staff from LCMS Concordia Seminary walk out to form Concordia Seminary in Exile, later Christ Seminary Seminex.

1974: The ALC and LCA begin World Hunger Appeals in response to famines in Africa.

1975: Stanley R. Goodwin and George Tinker are ordained as the first American Indian pastors.

1976: "Moderates" who left the Missouri Synods found the Association of Evangelical Lutheran Churches.

1978: *Lutheran Book of Worship* is published.

1978: AELC issues "Call to Union."

1980: LCA adopts the title bishop.

1982: ALC, LCA, and AELC conventions appoint seventy representatives to the Commission for a New Lutheran Church.

1983: Nelson Trout is the first African American Lutheran bishop in the United States.

1984: Will Herzfeld is the first African American bishop of an American Lutheran church body, the AELC.

1985: The Evangelical Lutheran Church in Canada is formed.

1986: ALC, AELC, and LCA conventions approve plans for a new church.

1987: The Evangelical Lutheran Church in America is formed by the AELC, the ALC, and the LCA.

1988: ELCA begins operations in Chicago on Jan. 1.

1990: St. Francis and First United Lutheran churches in San Francisco ordain openly gay pastors, contrary to ELCA policy, and are suspended for five years.

1991: ELCA Churchwide Assembly adopts a social statement on the death penalty and on abortion.

1992: April Ulring Larson is the first female Lutheran bishop in the United States.

1993: ELCA publishes first draft of the ELCA human sexuality statement; sensational media coverage leads to sharp controversy.

1997: ELCA Churchwide Assembly approves full communion with three Reformed churches but not with the Episcopal Church U.S.A.

1997: Addie Butler is the first African American elected as an ELCA officer.

1999: *The Joint Declaration on the Doctrine of Justification* is signed in Augsburg, Germany, by Lutheran and Roman Catholic leaders.

1999: ELCA Churchwide Assembly approves full communion with the Episcopal Church U.S.A. *(By 2000 both the ELCA and The Episcopal Church U.S.A. had approved the full communion relationship.)*

For reflection

1. Which of the changes in American Lutheranism during the twentieth century surprises you the most? Have you experienced this change firsthand?

2. The author outlines a number of changes that did not occur as anticipated. Which of these seems to have the greatest urgency today?

3. Looking ahead, imagine ten more changes that might define the life of the ELCA in the twenty-first century? Which of those seems most significant to you?

Section Four

Our Resilient Faith

Nine installments of a fourteen-part series that Lull was writing prior to his death in 2003.

21

A Church That Bounces Back

The death of Lutheranism? The reports are grossly exaggerated

Almost every week I hear from people who have been told that denominations have no future. Sometimes they report this with glee. Sometimes they break the news carefully, perceiving that I'm enthusiastic about being a Lutheran Christian.

I can never simply tell such folks that they are wrong. The future is unknown. Perhaps "Lutheran," "Catholic, "Episcopal," and "Reformed" have become meaningless realities. Denominational identity is unimportant to many who seek a church home. But as a historian I know that the death of Lutheranism has been predicted many times. There have been even harder struggles in the past than we experience today.

The worst of times may have been the decades after Martin Luther's death in 1546. The next year, Emperor Charles V and his armies marched against the Lutherans and soundly defeated them. He then attempted to reimpose Catholicism in the heart of Luther's own Saxony. Luther's friends fell out with each other. They held together as long as he lived, but they had different strategies for how to be faithful amid this persecution.

Eventually, Charles V failed in his attempt because Lutheranism had rooted itself too deeply to be forced out. The Lutheran church was tolerated, and Luther's followers were reconciled with each other by the *Formula of Concord* in 1577. But worse sufferings were to come.

In the Thirty Years War (1618-1648), Protestants and Catholics slaughtered each other in large numbers. The devastation in the Luther lands was especially severe. Peace and toleration finally came one hundred years after Luther's death, but Lutherans seemed spiritually exhausted and lacking in leadership.

Renewal came with the Pietist movement within Lutheranism in 1675. It re-established emphasis on strong biblical faith with personal commitment. Small-group gatherings in homes helped many laity articulate their faith. In the long run Pietism also had negative effects, introducing aspects of anti-clericalism and anti-intellectualism that still plague Lutheran churches.

Lutherans struggled to express their faith and organize their church as they moved out of Europe to all parts of the world. Early Lutheran settlers in North America puzzled about how to have a church if the government didn't provide it.

Many fell away to other denominations and revival movements that seemed to better fit the American experience. In the end, Lutherans met this challenge and learned how to organize the church in a more democratic way and how to raise money voluntarily to support its life and mission.

Perhaps the worst crisis of the past five hundred years was the complicity with the Nazi regime. While Dietrich Bonhoeffer, Martin Niemoeller, and others were heroes of the resistance, most German Lutherans went along with the government's murderous plans without much protest. This led many—within the Lutheran church and beyond—to wonder if Lutheranism was fatally flawed. They forgot that Lutherans in Denmark successfully resisted Adolf Hitler and worked together to save their Jewish neighbors.

The last fifty years have seen a worldwide rethinking of our theology and ethics. We have come to see that Luther's view of the relationship of church to government was more critical and creative than we'd previously thought.

This capacity to change in response to challenge continues today. The emergence of women as ordained pastors and as bishops is not complete and is still resisted in some parts of the Lutheran community. This and the rise of new voices of leadership from all parts of the world have given the Lutheran church a very different profile. Lutherans also have accepted the challenge of the modern ecumenical movement. We've had some surprising success, even resolving old differences with the Roman Catholic Church.

So I don't lose sleep over voices telling me that the end is near for denominations—and for Lutherans. Rather, I am curious to explore what Lutherans have going for them that has given them surprising resilience for more than five centuries. We have formidable resources that we scarcely understand, treasures in our Lutheran attic that are almost forgotten.

For reflection

1. Were you surprised to read about all the periods of challenge and renewal in Lutheran churches during the past five hundred years? Which historic period intrigues you the most?

2. What are the three most significant signs of challenge or renewal you have witnessed in your own lifetime?

22

A Large House, a Larger Attic

The Lutheran tradition has neglected options
waiting to be rediscovered

How shall we understand Lutheranism? Our church stretches back
over five centuries and extends around the world. I compare
Lutheranism to a very large house. If we think of the Lutheran
World Federation as us all living together, it's possible to imagine
how large the dwelling would have to be—with many different
rooms. It would include the traditional Lutheran churches of
Europe—German, Nordic, Hungarian, Baltic, and Slovak. It would
include the Lutherans of Canada and the United States, Africa,
Latin America, and Asia.

But you don't have to travel the world to experience diversity
within the Lutheran church. Even in your region, Lutherans probably worship in different ways, serve their neighbors in varying pat-
terns and build community in diverse ways. Some Lutherans look
more like Roman Catholics and some like Methodists. Lutherans
who have lived in different parts of the United States often
encounter these variations—sometimes to their shock, sometimes to
their delight.

Even in a congregation, the changes over time can be dramatic.
I recently visited the Lutheran church in Ohio where I grew up. I
have deep memories of the church—of the buildings and the
stained-glass windows, of people who are still active there decades
later. But a time traveler would be surprised to see the changes from
fifty years ago—from the hymns they sing to having women as pastors. These Lutherans—like most—have been able to change many
things while holding fast to what is good.

This capacity for change with continuity is partly grounded in the richness of our tradition. Envision Lutheranism as a very large house with an even larger attic—one from which many traditions and treasures can be brought down into the main rooms every time it's necessary to redecorate. The Lutheran tradition is so richly blessed with possibilities that it can't use all of them at the same time. We have old neglected options waiting to be rediscovered.

Imagine that this attic's rooms are filled with many kinds of material, especially two large rooms—one filled with great theological ideas and the other with great practical strategies. We could call these rooms the Noun Attic and the Verb Attic. They remind us that while rich theology has often been what makes Lutheranism great, there is also a case to be made for its practical genius—both of these tracing back to the Reformation.

During the next year, we'll explore our attic, examining these resources for renewal in our time. We'll encounter ideas such as Christian freedom and the theology of the cross; action strategies such as "to confess" and "to serve." Before we begin our survey, one interesting point emerges: If we have these multiple treasures, then we have no set starting point that all Lutherans must use for church reform. There is more than one way to refurnish the Lutheran house.

I often encounter people who tell me the Lutheran church turns them off. They say it's too gloomy or that they don't feel connected to justification by faith. For others it seems overly intellectual. Some find it ethically and socially passive. Some don't like Lutheran worship. How do we address these objections?

Beyond loyalty to the Lutheran confessions, Lutherans have considerable freedom in the concrete forms of church life. Much of our ability to bounce back from trouble and stagnation comes from these multiple resources. All the Lutheran themes and action strategies are connected, but there are different legitimate starting points and legitimate differences in emphases.

This allows us to be part of a community that has a distinct identity but also freedom and flexibility. Some insist their approach to being Lutheran is the only way and scorn others as "not really Lutheran." But this series is a celebration of the largeness of the Lutheran house and of the rich resources that we have hardly exhausted.

Lutheranism is one powerful version of how to be a Christian in today's world. In a season of giving and receiving, think of our Lutheran treasures as gifts waiting to be opened. That would make this a season of genuine joy and hope.

For reflection

1. How much variety and diversity have you experienced in the Lutheran congregations to which you have belonged or visited? Which experiences in those congregations have surprised you the most?

2. Which of the "treasures in the attic" (Lutheran theology, worship, teaching, or community life) is most important to you? How does your choice compare to the ones named by others?

23

Keys That Unlock the Bible

Luther's law/gospel distinction opens the Bible to us as a word of life

We compared Lutheranism to a large house with an even larger attic. As we explore the treasures of our tradition, we first discover a large ring of keys. These keys are a wonderful asset to open the greatest resource of all: The word of God found in the Bible, which contains our story and hope. But it's a large and confusing book that needs interpretation. It might as well be locked as far as many modern readers are concerned.

Martin Luther translated the Scriptures into the language of the people. But he never thought they would find Christian truth there without assistance. So he wrote Bible study helps and preaching resources to help people.

In Acts 8 the early Christian evangelist Philip meets an Ethiopian court official riding in his chariot. This man is reading the Scriptures—not unlike people I see on airplanes. Philip asks bluntly: "Do you understand what you are reading?" The Ethiopian's memorable answer could speak for all of us: "How can I unless someone guides me?"

The most important key on this large Lutheran ring is Luther's understanding of the difference between law and gospel. The law requires us to do certain things. But the gospel doesn't preach what we are to do or avoid. It sets up no requirements but reverses the approach of the law and says, "This is what God has done for you; he has let his Son be put to death for your sake" ("How Christians Should Regard Moses—1525": *Luther's Works*, Vol. 35:162).

Both law and gospel are the word of God for us and deserve attention. The fundamental mistake in most Bible reading is to see it all as law, a kind of moral manual for life. Then we become the center of the Bible story as we read it mostly to see what it is that God wants us to do.

Those who have learned to distinguish law from gospel don't neglect or dismiss the law. But they know that the Bible is fundamentally the story of God, of God's great work of creation, redemption, and reconciliation of the whole world. Other important things are secondary.

Such wise Bible readers also know that law is not the equivalent of the Old Testament, nor is gospel simply equated with the New. The Old Testament has some of the greatest words of promise in all of Scripture. The New Testament has some of the sharpest words of challenge, demand, and judgment. Luther never used the law/gospel distinction as an excuse to neglect the Old Testament. He found Christ there under words of promise and also found examples of living by faith unsurpassed even in the New Testament.

Another key on this large ring is Luther's notion of the "canon within the canon"—that certain biblical books are more important than others. These books take us to the central message—"drive us to Christ," as he often said. Luther's list included the Gospel of John; Paul's letters to the Romans, Galatians, and Ephesians; 1 Peter; and 1 John.

Luther has often been criticized for his impudence in declaring some Bible books more important than others. Perhaps he is more honest than his critics, for it seems most churches have a "canon within the canon" whether or not they use the term. Some evangelicals certainly make inordinate use of Daniel and Revelation. Some churches emphasize the teachings of Jesus and the Sermon on the Mount. But Luther's willingness to make distinctions about the importance of the various books sets us free to read the Bible as instructive in every part, but not with every verse and every book as important as all the others.

I try to talk to people who read the Bible on planes to see what they're reading and why. Often they're alienated from the church but still cling to the word. Often they have experienced an abuse of the Bible for human control, political agenda, or fund-raising that drove them away.

If Lutherans today have keys that can unlock the Scriptures, they have a great treasure indeed. Great hunger exists in our society among spiritually seeking people for an approach to the Bible that opens it up as a word of life and grace and hope. There is no greater tool for mission today than a credible approach to God's word.

For reflection

1. In your own words describe the distinction between law and gospel. Name a time when each played a crucial part in your relationship with God.

2. Which books of the Bible are on your own list as the most important keys to God's Word? How does your list compare to that of Martin Luther's?

24

God's Radical Work

Justification insists on God's utterly undeserved favor

Lutherans consider the Bible a great treasure with many themes. It presents the complex story of God's relationship to the world, a story of judgment and grace, demand and gift. But these aspects of God's relationship to humanity don't constitute a standoff, with law balancing gospel and sin balancing redemption. Our hope and confidence rest in the conviction that God is ultimately gracious and that our sins and brokenness are overcome by God's great love.

The term that expresses this bottom-line Lutheran conviction is *justification by faith* or, more completely, that we are "justified as a gift on account of Christ's sake through faith" (*Augsburg Confession*, IV). Justification is an image taken from the courtroom. We find it especially in Paul's letters. He compares God's action in Christ to the work of a judge who throws out the guilty verdict and sets the convicted prisoner free.

That image emphasizes the undeserved character of God's work on our behalf. Martin Luther taught early and often that we must first take Christ as a gift and only then as a teacher.

Paul further teaches that this active righteousness of God is a creative work of reconciliation. God not only rescues the wicked and estranged but also saves the good and the righteous from their bondage to the self. Part of the gospel's recurring shock is that the pious, the well-behaved, and those who attend church every Sunday need saving too.

This has always been controversial. It offended those who encountered Jesus' ministry among tax collectors and sinners. It was a centerpiece of the preaching of Paul and other early Christian missionaries who learned to welcome the gentiles. It was the basis of Luther's challenge to church practices that made the free gift of God unrecognizable.

Proud human beings may feel they need no saving at all. Even those who acknowledge their sin still want to do their part. Justification sweeps that all away. We humans stand together at the foot of Christ's cross, sinners perhaps in different degree and form, but all of us in a bondage from which we cannot free ourselves.

One can see justification in many Bible passages beyond Paul, where the word "justification" isn't used. The ancient prophets point to a future that rests not in the constancy of the people but in God's certain promise. In Luke 1, Mary sings of God's regard for the lowly. Jesus' parables are full of surprises as God's resolution of each story comes in an unexpected way.

What then must I do? Humans are responding creatures. We resist the notion that in the most important issue of our life—our relationship with God—God has already done what is needful. We are invited simply to trust God rather than ourselves, to walk each day resting our confidence in Christ and in all God's promises.

Sometimes, alas, Lutherans have been so anxious about faith that they made it into a new requirement. People were commanded "to believe" as if it were possible to fear, love, and trust in God just by trying hard. Luther taught otherwise. In the *Small Catechism* he wrote: "I believe that by my own understanding or strength I cannot believe in Jesus Christ my Lord or come to him."

Faith isn't the condition that completes the circuit and makes justification possible. Faith itself is a gift of the Spirit. Those who hear the good news of Jesus and long to live by faith must pray with the father of the epileptic boy: "I believe; help my unbelief!" (Mark 9:24).

Many Christians today, including some Lutherans, have no use for the most precious teaching of justification. They consider it outdated, too intellectual or too indifferent to human response. But our society is full of people struggling to hold their lives together by their own strength. They may not be trusting in good works, but they are trusting in hard work to assure the meaning of their lives. They, too, are in bondage.

We have something to offer them—if we have the courage to tell the story of God's radical love and to face the unsettling consequences it brings to our pride. Our churches are full of people who have never encountered justification in all its disarming and healing power.

For reflection

1. Describe a time in your life in which you have experienced God's gracious work of justification by faith at work in your own life. Why do many Christians have a difficult time perceiving God as the generous giver of reconciliation and faith itself?

2. How can you acknowledge and honor God's free gift of reconciliation in your life this week?

25

Luther's Great Discovery

Moments of defeat can be powerful occasions
for finding God's presence

When Martin Luther began to criticize church leaders for selling indulgences, he was also criticizing the way his fellow theologians did their work. Their heavy use of abstract philosophical terms wasn't the only barrier to understanding Christian truth. As professor of Scripture at Wittenberg University, Luther became convinced that teachers of his day did not really present the God of the Bible.

It was common to stress God's greatness and grandeur, the way God could be known by every mind simply by looking at the structure of creation itself. But they continued this stress on the big, the impressive, and the powerful even when it came to Christ and the church.

Jesus was the greatest teacher and best miracle worker. His resurrection topped the claims of any other faith. And the Roman Catholic Church itself was proclaimed to be true because of its impressive size and its spread throughout the world.

Luther called such reflections "theology of glory" that obscured the central Christian message. At the heart of our faith stands the story of Jesus who, at best, was temporarily acclaimed by the crowds. In the end he was despised and rejected. His crucifixion—by human standards—was a failure and a defeat.

But God chose just this moment of apparent failure and weakness to disclose the bottom line message for the world—love, grace, and mercy toward a lost humanity. God in Christ wasn't acting like the empire's powerful rulers or like the princes of the church. God was taking his place with the lowly, the marginal, those living under the shadow of death.

This is Luther's "theology of the cross." It doesn't just proclaim the death of Jesus for sinners, but even more God's judgment on the world's proud categories of what constitutes power and success. Luther read the Bible in light of the cross and saw a pattern of who God is and what God does, a pattern repeated from the beginning of the biblical story to its very end. The God we meet in Jesus isn't so much the God of power and might but more deeply the God whose ways are hidden and surprising.

In both the Old and New Testament, Luther found confirmation of the surprising way the true and living God deals with humanity, especially in Isaiah and in Paul. "For my thoughts are not your thoughts, nor are your ways my ways, says the Lord" (Isaiah 55:8). "We proclaim Christ crucified, a stumbling block to Jews and foolishness to Gentiles" (1 Corinthians 1:23). Jesus himself taught: "I thank you, Father, Lord of heaven and earth, because you have hidden these things from the wise and the intelligent and have revealed them to infants" (Matthew 11:25).

For Luther this "theology of the cross" was the clue about the right way to read the Bible and teach the Christian faith. It was also a powerful word of comfort and hope. In his thirty-year struggle leading the Reformation, Luther faced death several times. At other points his mistakes endangered the movement's success. The church and the empire regularly opposed and taunted him. But from the book of God's true dealings with humanity, he learned not to lose heart, to wait for God's surprising and hidden judgment.

Luther's theology of the cross has much to offer us. If God's version of success isn't the same as the world's bottom line, then we have reason to hope even when results are discouraging. We can press on even when we travel a lonely and difficult road. We should be wary of current spiritual self-help books that promise success without entering the narrow gate that leads to Calvary.

This understanding of God encourages us when things aren't going well personally. It also warns our churches not to jump to conclusions. We ought not gloat if things are going well but wait in prayer for God's verdict that our successes are a blessing, not simply a reward for giving the world whatever it wants spiritually.

We especially ought not lose heart when the church's future seems uncertain. Those, like Luther, who have deeply searched the Scriptures, know that even moments of defeat or abandonment can be powerful occasions for finding the presence of the true and living God.

For reflection

1. How do you define success in your own life? How is success measured and celebrated in your congregation? Are these examples of theology of glory or theology of the cross?

2. How have you learned to trust God from the perspective of *theology of the cross?*

26

Holy Extravagance

We should not try to renew the church by the spoken word alone

By the last ten years of Martin Luther's life (1536 to 1546), the Roman Catholic Church was taking the Reformation challenge very seriously. With a new pope (Paul III) in 1534, the church was planning to convene a general council. Earlier the reformers wanted this, hoping their complaints spoke for most Christians. Now they knew a council would likely try to crush their movement.

In the *Smalcald Articles* (1537), Luther wrote an account of the evangelical position. Stressing non-negotiable points, he reviewed their complaints about the mass, monastic orders and the papacy. He also powerfully articulated Lutheran convictions. His description of the gospel points to the diverse ways the good news comes to us:

> We now want to return to the gospel, which gives guidance and help against sin in more than one way, because God is extravagantly rich in his grace: first, through the spoken words, in which the forgiveness of sins is preached to the whole world (which is the proper function of the gospel); second, through baptism; third, through the holy Sacrament of the Altar; and fourth, through the power of the keys, and also through mutual conversation and consolation of brothers and sisters. (Part III, Article 4)

Luther understands that God's good news is an unlikely message. Every day we hear that "there is no free lunch" or that "God helps those who help themselves." The free grace of God's mercy toward all humanity is a surprise, and Luther knows we need to keep hearing it all our life.

What strikes him is God's extravagance. God brings us the gospel in many ways. Preaching stands first, as it had from the time of the apostles. It was a major Reformation achievement to renew preaching and return it to biblical focus and clarity. But the Lutheran plan was never to make everything rest on the sermon alone.

Luther also treasured baptism. Throughout his life he remembered that in it he became God's own dear child. His catechisms taught people to see baptism as God's deeply personal promise attached to their lives. Baptism was also the foundation of mature discipleship. In the course of a life, one slowly comprehends what it means to be marked with the seal of Christ forever.

He also criticized many practices of the mass in his day. But Luther treasured the Lord's Supper as another means of grace. He battled other reformers whom he thought gave too little weight to the rich promise of Christ's presence in the sacrament. He exhorted people to take communion even when they felt weak in faith.

Luther understood the eucharist as deeply communal. The blessings and benefits of Christ we receive empower a mutual exchange of the burdens and joys we bring to the Lord's table.

The way the church practiced penance troubled Luther, but he continued to consider confession and forgiveness a strong form of the gospel. Long after leaving the monastery, Luther regularly confessed his sins to the town pastor, John Bugenhagen. He knew the joy that came from speaking the truth about himself and the greater joy of forgiveness from God in the absolution.

Perhaps most surprising in Luther's *Smalcald* list is "mutual conversation and consolation" as a means of grace. He wasn't a member of a small group for prayer or Bible study in the modern sense. But he knew the ways grace comes from words ordinary Christians speak to one another—in church and in the fabric of daily activity.

Luther could be stormy in his theological writings, but he had a delicate touch when he wrote letters to many who had experienced great loss. He benefited from mutual conversation and offered it to his colleagues and neighbors as well.

The Lutheran church has seldom simultaneously valued all these gifts of our extravagant, imaginative God. We should not try to renew the church by the spoken word alone. We need to treasure all these forms that have been entrusted to us. In recent years we have made the sacraments more central in parish life and found wonderful ways to practice "mutual conversation."

Together, all these aspects of the church's life help us believe the gospel of a God who helps those who cannot help themselves.

For reflection

1. In the *Smalcald Articles* Luther articulates a number of ways in which God's good news comes to us. Describe several examples from your life in which you have experienced God's grace.

2. Which of these expressions of God's grace and mercy is most prominent in the congregation to which you belong?

27

Freedom and Vocation

Our world is full of people longing for fulfillment

Martin Luther challenged many standard practices for being a Christian in his day. He attacked indulgences and masses for the dead. He dismissed pilgrimages and veneration of the relics of the saints. He questioned whether several of the seven sacraments were truly sacraments. Soon the question arose among opponents and supporters: "If we don't do those things, how do we go about being Christians?"

Luther's answer came in several parts. He radically reinterpreted the Ten Commandments, presenting them not as a series of actions to be avoided but as clues about the positive things God wants us to do. It's not enough just to avoid killing—we're called to see that our neighbors have the things they need to live. It's not enough to avoid lying—we must put the most charitable construction on the things our neighbors do.

But the center of Christian living is found in the complex reality of Christian freedom. Here Luther drew especially on Galatians 5, noticing the importance of freedom—and its double edge.

On one hand the person who lives in Christ has been set free to be "lord of all, subject to none." Paul used this concept to defend the Gentile converts in Galatia from the demand that adult males be circumcised before they could join the church. Luther saw this freedom sweeping away many of the ritual actions that the church in his time demanded. Some of them might be acceptable pious practices. But when they were made requirements, the strong Pauline gospel needed to sound: "For freedom Christ has set us free. Stand firm, therefore, and do not submit again to a yoke of slavery" (Galatians 5:1).

But freedom is incomplete if it's only freedom *from* requirements. It finds its full realization as freedom *for* something. Luther argued that the same Christian who is "free lord of all" was at the same time "servant of all, subject to all." The glory of freedom is found in its completion as willing and voluntary service to one's neighbor.

But how can one be both "free lord" and "servant of all?" Luther's understanding of freedom is Christological. Jesus is the one who is both free Lord and willing servant. The great Christ hymn in Philippians 2 provides the clue: He who was equal with God found that equality wasn't something to be "exploited," but taking the form of the servant, humbled himself and became obedient. Jesus is the pattern for our Christian freedom.

This freedom has always frightened the church, whether it was encountering Paul's teaching or Luther. Our world is full of men and women longing for freedom—from parental control, from poverty, from oppression, from all forms of prejudice that marginalize so many. The church ought to see in those strivings for freedom something that it can affirm and support.

But the church also has an opportunity to teach that the deepest fulfillment is found in willing and voluntary service to others. Freedom as "no strings" may seem an improvement over a claustrophobic life, but it's also likely to end in loneliness, isolation, and disappointment.

Our vocation is a primary channel for the use of our freedom. Vocation is a personal calling, not simply an occupation. Luther closely linked freedom to vocation—his biblical conviction that all God's people are called to meaningful work in the world. God works through our diverse callings to serve the world's needs.

Today some long for a church that will tell them in detail just what their life as Christians must be. But I meet more people who are victims of bossy and controlling churches. Many unchurched feel they can only find freedom outside the church. When Lutherans claim their heritage of freedom and vocation, they have a powerful understanding of how Christians live in the world and a way to cheer for all those longing to be free.

To be credible in these teachings, the church has to avoid the ever-present temptation to think that it knows best, in detail, how each person should live. Jesus pointed another way when he told his disciples: "I do not call you servants any longer . . . but I have called you friends" (John 15:15). As friends of God in Christ, we practice self-restraint in telling each other how to live.

For reflection

1. If Martin Luther were to join you for a conversation what would you tell him about the longing for freedom in our own day?

2. Dr. Lull writes that "God works through our diverse callings to serve the world's needs." How might you describe your own sense of vocation through which you serve others?

28

Servant or Lord?

Luther's two kingdoms doctrine keeps the church focused on the gospel

From the beginning, the Reformation had a strong political aspect. Martin Luther insisted that he wasn't starting a revolution, but his challenge to the authority of the church quickly brought him into conflict with popes and princes. The ensuing thirty-year struggle (1517-1547) was framed by the rising power of Islam in Eastern Europe. No one could have imagined the final outcome—with various Christian confessions living side by side in neighboring territories.

In Luther's time many bishops also ruled extensive realms. The pope controlled central Italy and was deeply involved in protecting his domain. Pope Julius II (died 1513) personally led his troops into battle. The papacy struggled to maintain a balance of power among Spain, England, France, the Holy Roman Empire, and others. This often led the church to preoccupation with political matters and blindness to its faults.

Luther believed such direct political control was very bad for the churches. The proper work of the ministry—the preaching of the gospel and the sharing of the sacraments—was neglected in favor of maintaining the church's power.

He originally saw princes as allies in the reform of the church. Luther's rulers in Saxony were exceptional. In 1520 he invited the German nobles to become "emergency bishops" since the regular bishops wouldn't act to help the church. Later he saw that even good princes could meddle in church affairs. Their concerns were very different from the pastoral needs of the people.

Luther slowly clarified his notion of the two kingdoms or two realms, building on the concept of the two swords (church and government) in the writing of Augustine. But his thought flowed most directly from ongoing study of the Bible. There he saw that God works not only through religious communities but also through government. In Isaiah even a pagan king can be "God's servant" through whom the divine will is accomplished (Isaiah 45). Early Christians prayed for the emperors, even those who persecuted them.

The bottom line for Christians is the story of the world's redemption in Jesus Christ. But God is not only the redeemer but also the creator, who continued to give life and order to the world. Luther's *Small Catechism* speaks about creation in present tense verbs: "God daily and abundantly provides shoes and clothing, food and drink, house and farm, spouse and children, fields, livestock and all property—along with all the necessities and nourishment for this body and life."

Among those necessities of life is government, which may be better or worse, but is always a potential instrument for maintaining order and doing good.

This insight led Luther to respect non-Christians who governed justly and to be critical of Christians who assumed they did God's will simply because they were part of the church. He told those who wanted Germany to be a Christian nation that they should find a few real Christians first. Christians can cooperate with others in feeding the hungry and working for peace and justice, even if these others do not share our faith. This also means that politics—so derided in our culture—is an honorable vocation through which men and women may express their discipleship for the needs of the neighbor.

The two kingdoms doctrine focuses the church on its basic task of seeing that the gospel doesn't get lost in the busyness of life. Luther never intended that his two kingdoms idea would keep the church from "speaking about politics." His sermons are full of challenges to the princes, town councils and citizens about political matters. He blasted the town councils of Germany for their reluctance to raise enough taxes for schools.

But the heart of the church's life is easily lost if it aspires to direct political rule. It has been given the task of witness and service, not of domination and lordship (Matthew 20:20–28).

When someone asked Jesus about whether it was lawful to pay taxes, he replied: "Give to the emperor the things that are the emperor's, and to God the things that are God's." Each generation must struggle to determine the boundaries of just what belongs to governing authority and what belongs to God alone.

For reflection

1. In the twenty-first century what is the proper role of the church and the proper role of the government in our own culture?

2. Can you describe an experience in which a non-Christian neighbor helped you or others in your community at a crucial time? How does that example illustrate a Lutheran understanding of *two kingdoms*?

29

To Confess

Testifying to our faith amid resistance
has made Lutheranism resilient

For months we've explored one part of the Lutheran attic—the great theological concepts like justification and Christian freedom for which our tradition is famous. But if you step across the hall in the imaginary house of Lutheranism, you enter a different room. There we discover that the Reformation wasn't just about ideas and the mind. Part of the resilience of this tradition is that it has a whole set of verbs—action strategies for how to be the church in God's world.

The first of these verbs is "to confess." You likely want to complete the phrase with the words "to confess . . . our sins." That is an important Lutheran activity. We don't live under an illusion that human beings are problem free. We need confession and absolution. But the meaning I explore here is "to confess . . . one's faith."

On one level this is a common Christian practice. We recite the basic Christian story as we confess the Apostles' or Nicene creeds at Sunday worship. But we find the origins of confessing in the experience of the early Christians who were taking their stand with a new religious movement not authorized by the Roman Empire.

Peter, Paul, and most of the other apostles were martyrs. They not only died for the faith but witnessed to it by refusing to renounce it even on threat of death. These men and woman were the first Christian confessors. They are our forebearers in the faith whenever we take our active stand with the Christian community.

During the Reformation, confession of faith became particularly necessary—not in the face of persecuting Roman emperors but of certain officials of the Roman Catholic Church who wouldn't tolerate what they saw as a dangerous new religious movement.

Martin Luther's followers considered themselves loyal Christians who were holding to the ancient teachings on Christ, grace and faith. Luther's brave "Here I stand" confession before Emperor Charles V had to be repeated in varying contexts and by different people over the next few decades as the pressures to "return to Rome" continued. The first Lutheran martyrs were Augustinians Henry Vos and John van den Esschen, who were burned at the stake in Brussels July 1, 1523, by Charles' agents.

Many of these confessors were theologians. Their writings—along with the ancient creeds of the church catholic—make up the *Book of Concord,* the official confessions of the Lutheran church (Fortress Press, 1959). Such witnessing was not just an academic enterprise. Local pastors, town councils, princes, and ordinary Christians often had to make a choice to side with the Reformation and against "the way we've always done it." This was sometimes costly—loss of privilege, banishment, or even death. Along with Luther and his colleague Philip Melanchthon, these men and women are our forebearers in the practice of confessing the faith.

In our society, the peril of being a confessor seems small in comparison to the risks taken by early Christians, in the Reformation period, or in parts of the world today where Christians experience persecution. But confessing remains a central missional practice of the church.

Today men and women are drawn to the church by the testimony, courage, and integrity of ordinary Christians who give an account of their faith. This is especially inspiring and highly credible to those on the outside looking in.

Being a Lutheran Christian today is perhaps a riskier matter than we think. Our understanding of grace and freedom, Jesus' teachings on possessions or violence, and the hope beyond death that Christians hold, all set us against many of our society's principalities and powers.

Our society often admires religion so long as it is private and uncontroversial, which isn't faithful Christianity. Theologian Douglas John Hall wrote that we become confessors today when "we are thrust into an active engagement with that which threatens the life of our world" (*Confessing the Faith,* Fortress Press, 1998).

The paths of discipleship inevitably lead us to those places where our neighbors are in need, where we likely have to learn again what it means "to confess."

For reflection

1. In your own words describe what it means to confess the faith. Can you remember a time in your life when you did just that?

2. The early Christian martyrs died confessing their faith in Jesus Christ. What do you hope others will say about you as a "confessor of the faith" at the time of your death?

Afterword

Tim Lull traveled extensively, preaching and speaking to the people of the church at synod assemblies, pastoral convocations, and in the Sunday morning gatherings of the faithful. These essays reflect many of his concerns, as well as his deep love for the work and mission of the church.

During those travels Tim was always running into people who had heard him speak. He would return home, his spirits buoyed not because someone had remembered his words but because others shared his hopeful convictions about God's continuing work through the church. These essays, which first appeared in *The Lutheran*, were written to nourish that spirit of hope. They still speak to us today.

Tim died suddenly in May 2003. Earlier that spring in a letter to his family he wrote, "I intend to die confessing faith in the Triune God in whose name I was baptized so many years ago, with the deepest gratitude for the blessings of family, friends, and vocation which have been mine, and with wonder at the great richness of the life I have been privileged to live." We hope that these essays serve as a testimony to that contemporary confession of the faith and as an encouragement for you to do the same.

Mary Carlton Lull
Patricia J. Lull